Fugitive Slave on Trial

Paul:

This is what I do
because I don't have a
jump shot!

Best wishes,

Earl Grint

LANDMARK LAW CASES

AMERICAN SOCIETY

Peter Charles Hoffer
N. E. H. Hull
Series Editors

EARL M. MALTZ

Fugitive Slave on Trial

The Anthony Burns Case and

Abolitionist Outrage

UNIVERSITY PRESS OF KANSAS

Published by the University Press of Kansas (Lawrence, Kansas 66045), which was
organized by the Kansas Board of Regents and is operated and funded by Emporia
State University, Fort Hays State University, Kansas State University, Pittsburg State
University, the University of Kansas, and Wichita State University

Library of Congress Cataloging-in-Publication Data

Maltz, Earl M., 1950–
Fugitive slave on trial : the Anthony Burns case and abolitionist outrage /
Earl M. Maltz.
p. cm. — (Landmark law cases & American society)
Includes bibliographical references and index.
ISBN 978-0-7006-1735-7 (cloth : alk. paper)
ISBN 978-0-7006-1736-4 (pbk. : alk. paper)
1. Fugitive slaves — Legal status, laws, etc. — United States. 2. Burns, Anthony,
1834–1862 — Trials, litigation, etc. 3. Fugitive slaves — Legal status, laws, etc. —
Massachusetts. 4. Loring, Edward G. (Edward Greely), 1802–1890. I. Title.
KF4545.S5M353 2010
342.7308'7 — dc22
2010018068

British Library Cataloguing-in-Publication Data is available.

Printed in the United States of America

10 9 8 7 6 5 4 3 2 1

As always, for my family

CONTENTS

In 1854, Virginia slave Anthony Burns stowed away on a ship bound for Boston Harbor and, he hoped, his freedom. His master discovered Burns's plan and arranged for him to be recaptured in Boston. There, according to the Fugitive Slave Act of 1850, he would be detained and brought before a federal commissioner, who could not fail to be convinced that Burns must be returned to Virginia and slavery. But Boston was the hub of the Anti-Slavery Society. Once despised and harassed, the abolitionists now had powerful friends, and a rescue of Burns nearly succeeded.

The stage was set for a unique test of law — the hearing that would determine Burns's fate. The hero (or antihero) of this part of the tale is the commissioner, one Edward Loring. His views were as conflicted as the nation itself. Although he made an effort to buy Burns's freedom, Loring was no abolitionist. A conservative Whig at a time when fewer and fewer politicians constrained their sectional allegiances, he wished for a quiet life and a quick solution to the Burns affair. But he was also a man who believed in the rule of law, and for him, due process meant giving both sides in the case time and space to make their arguments. And those arguments would contain ironies aplenty. The briefs and the ruling recapitulated the legal arguments of nearly two generations of advocates of slavery and freedom, respectively, and anticipated the briefs in the *Dred Scott* case. Loring would be subjected to a torrent of abuse. In the end, the case of one runaway slave captured the attention of the entire nation.

But law professor and historian Earl Maltz is not just a storyteller, although the story here is as dramatic and compelling as any in our legal annals. He locates the Burns case in an argument over slavery and freedom going back to the Constitution's rendition clause, then follows it through two iterations of federal statutes in 1793 and 1850, a miniature legal war between the governors of Massachusetts and Virginia, and the reappearance of the Boston mob (shades of the Sons of Liberty, with the abolitionist Vigilance Committee of 1854 reenacting the role of the revolutionary "Loyal Nine" of 1765) rescuing runaways held in the local jails — complete with a near-reprise of the Boston Massacre and the abolitionists' violent resistance to federal law. The trial of Anthony Burns and the consequent trials of Edward Loring revealed that there was little ground for compromise when it came to slavery, even years before Abraham Lincoln spoke of a "house divided" and William Henry Seward warned of an "irrepressible conflict."

In this essay, as in his earlier work for the series, Maltz shows something of Loring's best qualities — intellectual honesty and the determination to be fair-minded. Maltz is a master of legal detail and an astute observer of contemporary politics with a deft literary touch. The result is a fascinating and deeply disturbing account of a nation moving inexorably toward sectional division. Only law — respect for law, wise and prudent law, and the abilities of the nation's lawyers and judges — might save the nation from falling into that chasm.

Introduction

The 1854 rendition of Anthony Burns was one of the most dramatic and widely publicized incidents in the long-running conflict over the issue of fugitive slaves in the antebellum era. At the time that Burns stowed away on a ship in Norfolk, Virginia, in early 1854, he was no doubt concerned only with improving his personal situation. But when Charles F. Suttle, his erstwhile master, discovered Burns's whereabouts and tracked him to Boston, the struggle over Burns's fate became front-page news and a focal point not only in the sectional conflict between the North and the South but also in the internecine conflict for control of the Massachusetts state government.

Edward Greely Loring was at the epicenter of this struggle over Burns's fate and the political battle that followed. Prior to 1854, no one would have predicted that Loring would play an important role in a significant incident in American history. Although he was a relative by marriage to the formidable Curtis family and moonlighted as a lecturer at Harvard Law School, most of Loring's time was occupied with his duties as a probate judge. As such, he typically dealt with matters far removed from the political turmoil of the day. Thus, most contemporary observers would have predicted that Loring would live out the rest of his days in relative obscurity.

However, Loring's life changed dramatically on May 25, 1854, when, in his capacity as a commissioner of the local federal district court, he was called on to adjudicate the claim that Anthony Burns was the property of Virginia slave owner Charles F. Suttle. At first, it seemed that the matter might be resolved quickly against Burns. But that possibility disappeared after Loring granted a postponement to allow antislavery attorneys time to prepare a defense. The events of the tumultuous week that followed included a violent rescue attempt that resulted in the death of one of the men guarding the courthouse and a concerted but ultimately unsuccessful effort to purchase Burns's freedom prior to a formal resolution of his status. Equally significant was the course of the hearing itself, for against all odds, Burns's attorneys were able to produce evidence that the man who had been brought before Loring was not in fact a fugitive slave.

Loring was thus presented with a dilemma. Certainly, nothing in the historical record suggests that Loring was anxious to remand Burns to Suttle's custody. Loring was an active participant in the effort to purchase Burns's freedom, and no objective observer would conclude that Loring's conduct of the hearing showed any bias in favor of Suttle. Moreover, Loring was clearly aware that a decision against Burns would be harshly criticized by many prominent elements in Boston society.

But at the same time, Loring was not a fervent believer in the antislavery cause. Even in the wake of the political upheaval attending the dispute over the Kansas-Nebraska Act, he remained an unrepentant conservative Whig who supported the Compromise of 1850 in general and enforcement of the Fugitive Slave Act, which was an intrinsic part of that compromise, in particular. Loring was also by all appearances deeply committed to what might be described as the ideology of law—the idea that each individual case should be decided by reference to "neutral" principles, without considering overtly political factors. And so, on Friday, June 2, Loring ordered that Burns be remanded to the custody of Suttle and returned to Virginia—a decision that was indisputably correct on the facts and almost certainly justified by existing legal precedent.

The immediate consequences for Burns were both predictable and catastrophic. He was returned to Virginia under armed guard, and Suttle soon sold him to a new master in North Carolina. Fortunately, Burns's reenslavement was short-lived. Through a combination of good fortune and the assiduous efforts of the Reverend Leonard A. Grimes, Burns's freedom was purchased, and he returned to Boston as a freeman in March 1855.

Loring, however, became a prime target for the wrath of the politically powerful antislavery forces in Boston and throughout the state of Massachusetts. He lost his post at Harvard and was the subject of an aggressive, sustained campaign to remove him from the Massachusetts bench. Ironically, at a dramatic series of legislative hearings in 1855, Loring's most visible defender was Richard Henry Dana, who had been the lead attorney for Burns in the rendition proceedings that gave rise to the controversy over Loring's future. Although the initial effort to remove Loring failed, his foes persisted until they were finally successful in 1858. This book is the story of the trial of Anthony Burns and the trials of Edward Loring — both the rendition hearing over which he presided and the removal proceedings in which he was essentially the defendant.

CHAPTER I

The Problem of Fugitive Slaves, 1787–1841

For much of the pre–Civil War era, disputes over the treatment of fugitive slaves were a major source of tension between the Northern and Southern states. Escapees from bondage in the slave states often sought refuge in the North, either permanently or en route to Canada. Southerners complained that Northern residents interfered unduly with efforts to apprehend these fugitives, while some Northerners asserted that free blacks were too often kidnapped and sent into slavery under the pretense of being escapees. In constitutional terms, the dispute focused on the proper interpretation of article IV, section 2, paragraph 3 – the Fugitive Slave Clause.

The Fugitive Slave Clause was the most unambiguously pro-slavery provision to emerge from the Constitutional Convention of 1787. To be sure, many commentators have argued that a number of other sections of the Constitution favored Southern interests. However, the Fugitive Slave Clause was the only provision that explicitly granted slave owners rights that they had not previously possessed. Under the Articles of Confederation, each state could, if it wished, free any putative slave found within its borders. By contrast, the new Constitution both forbade states from declaring escaped slaves free and guaranteed slave owners the right to recover runaways.

Nonetheless, at the time it was adopted, the clause itself was almost entirely uncontroversial. On August 28, 1787, after the convention had committed itself to a provision requiring states to extradite fugitives from justice, Pierce Butler and Charles Pinckney of South Carolina moved to require "fugitive slaves and servants to be delivered up like criminals." James Wilson of Pennsylvania observed that "this would require the executive of the state to do it, at public expense," and Roger Sherman of Connecticut complained that he "saw no more propriety in the public seizing and surrendering a slave or a servant than a horse." Butler then withdrew his motion "in order that some particular provision might be made, apart from [the Extradition Clause]." On August 29 his motion to insert a separate clause was adopted without objection, and on September 12 the Committee on Style and Arrangement produced language that was essentially identical to that which is currently in the Constitution. After a minor change in wording on September 15, the Fugitive Slave Clause became part of the convention's proposal, without apparent dissent.

This new protection for slaveholders played little role in the struggle over ratification. Some Southern Federalists did point to the clause as a benefit to the South. However, the reaction of Northern Anti-Federalists stood in marked contrast to their treatment of other provisions of the new Constitution that they viewed as pro-slavery. While Northern opponents of the Constitution vociferously attacked both the apportionment of the House of Representatives and the Slave Trade Clause, their reaction to the Fugitive Slave Clause was, with few exceptions, a resounding silence.

To some modern observers, this lack of discussion might seem odd. But the basic concept underlying the Fugitive Slave Clause was by no means novel. As early as 1643, the New England Confederation had mandated intercolonial cooperation in the rendition of fugitive slaves. Moreover, by the time the Constitutional Convention met in Philadelphia, the possibility of conflict over the issue had been greatly magnified by the developing sectional divide over the issue of slavery more generally. The drafters of the Constitution faced a situation in which the momentum of the emancipation movement was accelerating in the Northern states, while support for the institution of slavery remained strong in the South, particularly the Deep South. Further, by 1787, Massachusetts had already become a refuge for runaways from the South. In the absence of some constitutional provision to the contrary, as slavery was abolished in other states, they too might become such refuges, inevitably creating sectional tensions that could threaten the unity of the nation. The lack of opposition to the Fugitive Slave Clause suggests that unionists of all stripes accepted the need to forestall this danger.

In short, unlike provisions such as the Three-fifths Clause and the Slave Trade Clause, the Fugitive Slave Clause was not a sectional compromise between delegates who began with opposing conceptions of the appropriate course of action. Instead, it was the embodiment of a basic premise that underlay the long-term success of any union between the Northern and Southern states. Even by the late eighteenth century, when slavery remained legal in most of the Northern states, it had become clear that the economic and social system in the South was based on principles quite different from those that prevailed in the North. Union between North and South was simply not plausible if the governments of the North were committed to undermining the slavery-based systems of the South. In essence, the Fugitive Slave Clause defined the minimum degree of tolerance for Southern institutions that the slave states required of Northern states.

At the same time, the language chosen for the clause created a variety of interpretational difficulties. Despite the protestations of Roger Sherman, the wording of the Fugitive Slave Clause was clearly patterned on that of the Extradition Clause. Both clauses were premised on the theory that the state from which the alleged fugitive came was the proper venue for determining his ultimate status. Conversely, the function of the government of the state in which he was found was simply to detain the alleged fugitive and deliver him to the appropriate party.

However, the two clauses differed in one critical respect. Fugitives from justice are alleged to have offended against the public order. Thus, the Constitution requires that the request for extradition be made by the "executive authority" of the state from which the fugitive allegedly fled. Under normal circumstances, one would not expect a governor to make such a request unless a criminal prosecution had been begun in good faith against the fugitive, and one would expect that the charges against the fugitive would be adjudicated by a criminal court after his extradition.

By contrast, any invocation of the right to recover a fugitive slave inevitably implicated a more complex set of interests. In the case of a putative slave, the claimant would not be a government official but a private party who had a pecuniary interest in the assertion of a right to hold that person to service. This incentive created the specter of Southerners possibly invoking the constitutional mandate in support of dubious claims or even enlisting the aid of Northern state governments in outright kidnapping schemes. Conversely, antislavery Northerners seized on the need to protect free blacks as justification for state laws that placed obstacles in the path of those seeking the return of blacks who were "fugitives from service." These issues provided the backdrop for congressional action in the early 1790s.

Ironically, the sequence of events that led to passage of the Fugitive Slave Act of 1793 began with the kidnapping of a free black man, John Davis. Sometime in the 1770s, while Davis was still a slave, his master had brought him from Maryland to what he believed to be part of Virginia. At the time, however, the border between Virginia and Pennsylvania was uncertain, and on August 31, 1779, representatives of the two states determined that the area in which the Davises had settled was in fact part of Pennsylvania. Although the agreement was not finally ratified until April 1, 1784, both John Davis and his master became subject to the provisions of Pennsylvania's Gradual Emancipation Act of 1780.

Under the terms of that statute, all children born to slaves in Pennsylvania after March 1, 1780, became free after a period of indenture. Masters were allowed to retain all slaves they owned in Pennsylvania as of March 1, 1780, provided the slaves were registered with a court clerk prior to November 1, 1780. All slaves not so registered became free immediately. In 1782, recognizing the uncertainties faced by slave owners in areas previously claimed by Virginia, the Pennsylvania legislature amended the statute to give those slave owners until January 1, 1783, to register their slaves.

John Davis's master did not take advantage of the registration opportunity, and in 1788 he hired John out to a Mr. Miller in Virginia. Some of John's neighbors, purportedly members of the Pennsylvania Abolition Society, found him in Virginia and returned with him to Pennsylvania. Miller then hired Francis McGuire, Baldwin Parsons, and Absalom Wells — all Virginians — to bring John back to Virginia. The three men succeeded in locating John and forcibly returned him in May 1788. John was then sold to a planter in eastern Virginia.

In November 1788 McGuire, Parsons, and Wells were indicted for kidnapping in Pennsylvania state court. In June 1791, at the request of the Pennsylvania Abolition Society, Pennsylvania governor Thomas Mifflin sent Virginia governor Beverly Randolph a copy of the indictment and a request for extradition of the three accused men. Randolph referred the request to James Innes, the state attorney general. Innes responded with a report concluding that, for a variety of reasons, the

Extradition Clause of the federal Constitution did not require Randolph to grant the request. Relying on this report, Randolph sent a formal refusal to Mifflin in July 1791.

Mifflin then appealed for aid to President George Washington, who referred the matter to Attorney General Edmund Randolph. Attorney General Randolph concluded that the initial request for extradition had been technically deficient, but that if these deficiencies were remedied, Governor Randolph should extradite the fugitives. Mifflin then sent a new request with the changes suggested by the attorney general. Nonetheless, the Virginia governor still refused to cooperate, in part because state legislators from McGuire's district complained that John Davis was in fact a slave who had been lured from Virginia by members of the Pennsylvania Abolition Society; as such, the case involved nothing more than prosecution for the justifiable recapture of a fugitive slave. Thus, rather than granting the extradition request, Governor Randolph complained to Governor Mifflin that Pennsylvanians were "seducing and harboring the slaves of the Virginians."

The dispute over John Davis provided the background for congressional action on both the extradition of fugitives from justice and the recovery of fugitive slaves. On October 27, 1791, President Washington sent Congress copies of both his correspondence with Governor Mifflin and the report prepared by Attorney General Randolph. On October 31 the House of Representatives referred the issue to a committee composed of three members: Theodore Sedgwick and Sherarjashbub Bourne of Massachusetts and Alexander White of Virginia. The committee was charged with preparing a bill that provided the means for both the extradition of fugitives and the rendition of fugitive slaves. On November 15 Sedgwick reported a bill that addressed both issues.

Under the procedures established by the bill, one who sought to recover a putative fugitive slave could present an application to the governor of the state in which the alleged fugitive was found. The application was required to be supported by the depositions of two persons who affirmed that the person identified was in fact a fugitive slave. Upon receipt of such an application, the governor was instructed to issue an arrest warrant, which would be enforced by the appropriate officials. After being arrested, the alleged fugitive would be delivered to the person who had applied for the warrant. State officials who refused to enforce such arrest warrants would have been subject to stiff fines in federal court.

The Sedgwick bill was read twice on November 15 and scheduled for a third reading. However, for unknown reasons, the third reading never took place, and the bill died without a vote. The following year the Senate took the lead. In March 1792 a committee comprising George Cabot of Massachusetts, Roger Sherman of Connecticut, and Ralph Izard of South Carolina was appointed to consider the issues of the extradition of fugitives from justice and the rendition of fugitive slaves. At the beginning of the next session, the Senate appointed a new committee consisting of Cabot, George Read of Delaware, and Samuel Johnston of North Carolina to consider the same subject. On December 20 the new committee reported a bill that was in some respects more favorable to claimants than the proposal that had died the previous year in the House of Representatives. The Senate bill required state officials to arrest and turn over alleged fugitive slaves on the basis of a single deposition. Under the bill, law enforcement agents who refused to aid claimants were subject to fines, and any private citizen who "harboured" or "concealed" a fugitive slave was subject to a penalty for each day he aided the fugitive. Claimants were also granted the right to sue those who aided fugitives for damages.

After debate, on December 28, the Senate returned the bill to a committee that was expanded to include Sherman and John Taylor of Virginia. On January 3, 1793, the reconfigured committee reported a bill that was radically different from the December 20 proposal. Although it allowed owners or their agents to seize putative runaways without first obtaining government permission, the new bill required anyone seized as a fugitive slave to be brought before a judge or magistrate before being removed from the state. In most cases, a certificate of removal would be granted if the claimant provided "proof to the satisfaction" of the presiding officer, in the form of either sworn testimony or an affidavit. However, no such certificate would be granted if the alleged fugitive had been a resident of the state for a certain number of years. In that case, the putative runaway could be removed only after a jury trial in the state in which he was found. Like the December 20 bill, the January 3 bill provided for monetary damages against law enforcement officials who failed to cooperate in the rendition process, as well as fines and imprisonment for private citizens who interfered with claimants' efforts to recover fugitives.

Although the precise content of the discussions was not recorded, the January 3 bill was apparently very controversial. Between January 14 and January 16, the Senate reconfigured the bill into a form that was more acceptable to both sides of the debate. In this form, the bill passed the Senate on January 18. The House of Representatives passed the bill in a slightly amended form on February 4, and the Senate concurred in the House amendment on the same day. On February 12, 1793, President George Washington signed the bill into law.

Under the Fugitive Slave Act of 1793, a slave owner or his agent was "empowered to seize or arrest [the] fugitive from labour" and bring him before a federal judge or "any magistrate of a county, city or town corporate" where the fugitive had been found. Upon "proof to the satisfaction" of the official, which could be provided by either affidavit or oral testimony, the official was required to issue a certificate that allowed the claimant to remove the alleged fugitive from the state where he was found to the state from which he had allegedly escaped. Any person who concealed a runaway or interfered with efforts to recover a fugitive was subject to a $500 penalty, payable to the slave owner.

Neither side was entirely satisfied with the regime established by the 1793 statute. Many Southerners believed that the law provided insufficient protection for the rights of slave owners. Some Northerners, in contrast, argued that free blacks in the North were left vulnerable to being kidnapped and sent into slavery. Advocates of these positions sought to have their concerns addressed by additional legislation at both the federal and state levels. Nonetheless, the 1793 statute remained unchanged for more than half a century, providing a backdrop for the evolution of the dispute over fugitive slaves more generally.

This dispute did not play a significant role in Massachusetts politics in the early nineteenth century. Unlike some other Northern states, prior to 1837 the state legislature made no effort to pass laws specifically designed to protect those who were alleged to be fugitives from service. However, a person seized on an allegation that he was an escaped slave could still invoke more generally available legal remedies.

10   { *Chapter 1* }

The background of the 1823 decision in *Commonwealth v. Griffith* illustrates this point. *Griffith* revolved around the effort to recover John Randolph, a slave who had fled from Virginia to Bedford, Massachusetts. Camillus Griffith, acting as the agent of Randolph's owner, seized Randolph without a warrant and placed him in confinement, pending a hearing before a magistrate on the question of whether a certificate of removal should be granted. Griffith was then indicted and convicted in state court of both false imprisonment and assault and battery.

On appeal, the Supreme Judicial Court was forced to confront a challenge to the constitutionality of the Fugitive Slave Act. Griffith interposed the statute as a defense, noting that the act explicitly authorized the seizure of a fugitive slave for the purpose of obtaining a certificate of removal. However, the prosecution argued that this provision violated the Fourth Amendment, with Attorney General Perez Morton noting that under the law of Massachusetts, Randolph was "*prima facie* a freeman, and entitled to all rights of a freeman, until it should have been proved in legal manner that he was a slave." By contrast, Griffith's attorney scoffed at the idea that any Fourth Amendment rights were implicated, noting that "the clause against unreasonable searches and seizures does not protect a slave" and asking, "where is the danger in allowing a master to seize his slave [without a warrant] in another State? . . . If [the putative master] seizes a freeman, he does it at his peril. He cannot plead a mistake in the person. He must prove his property fully [in any subsequent judicial proceeding]."

With only one dissent, the court reversed the lower court judgment and freed Griffith. Speaking for the court, Chief Justice Isaac Parker began by asserting that, because the Fugitive Slave Clause does not outline the processes to be used in the rendition of fugitive slaves, the mode of enforcing the clause was left to the discretion of Congress. Turning specifically to the Fourth Amendment issue, the opinion echoed the arguments for the defense, observing that any freeman mistakenly or deliberately seized under the color of this statute could obtain relief through a writ of habeas corpus and noting, "whether the statute is a harsh one, is not for us to determine."

The use of habeas corpus provided the background for a more widely reported incident that took place in Boston on August 3, 1836.

The dispute revolved around the status of two African American women, Eliza Small and Polly Ann Bates, both of whom had arrived in Boston from Baltimore on the brig *Chickasaw* on July 30. Both women were alleged to be enslaved to John B. Morris, who designated Matthew Turner as his agent to return Small and Bates to Maryland. When the *Chickasaw* arrived in Boston, Turner boarded the brig and confronted the two women. Contemporary accounts of the events that followed, though not entirely inconsistent, are at least somewhat confusing. Some newspapers reported that Small and Bates "readily admitted" they were escaped slaves. Others insisted that Small and Bates carried documentation of their free status and that when one of them proffered her papers to Turner, he refused to return them. But one point is clear: at Turner's request, Henry Eldridge, captain of the *Chickasaw*, agreed to detain Small and Bates to give Turner the opportunity to obtain a warrant to bring them before a federal judge for a hearing, as provided by the Fugitive Slave Act.

As news of the situation spread, a crowd gathered around the brig. At the same time, Samuel H. Adams, an African American Bostonian, petitioned Chief Justice Lemuel Shaw for a writ of habeas corpus to force Eldridge to bring the women into court to test the legality of their confinement. For technical reasons, the hearing on the writ was postponed until August 3. On that date, appearing before a packed courtroom on behalf of Captain Eldridge and, by extension, Turner, attorney A. H. Fiske presented an affidavit from Turner stating that Small and Bates were in fact slaves owned by Morris. In addition, Fiske launched a spirited defense of the Fugitive Slave Act and requested that the hearing be postponed to allow the production of additional evidence from Baltimore to support the claimant's position. Abolitionist attorney Samuel Eliot Sewall responded by arguing that, even granting the constitutionality of the Fugitive Slave Act, the statute did not give Eldridge the authority to detain the two women.

Shaw ruled that Eldridge had no right to detain Small and Bates. Turner then rose and indicated that he wished to invoke the Fugitive Slave Act and rearrest the two women. He asked whether a warrant was needed for that purpose. As Turner spoke, a constable was sent to lock the doors to the courtroom. But before Shaw could answer Turner, Sewall reportedly beckoned to the crowd, and the spectators surged forward and bodily removed Small and Bates from the courtroom over Shaw's vehement objections, manhandling the courtroom sheriff in the process and pushing a constable down a flight of stairs. Small and Bates were then shoved into a carriage and carried out of town, with their screaming rescuers following.

These events were reported in a variety of newspapers throughout the nation, with commentators generally voicing shock and anger. For example, the *Boston Atlas* described the *Chickasaw* affair as an "outrageous violation of justice," and the *Boston Transcript* characterized the actions of the crowd as a "gross outrage." Moreover, George Adams — a naval lieutenant who was also a relative of John Morris — was not content with simple verbal condemnation. On September 8 Adams appeared at Sewall's office and requested a private meeting. After castigating Sewall for his role in the escape of Small and Bates, Adams struck the abolitionist lawyer with the butt of a whip. A struggle ensued, which ended only after others intervened to physically separate the two men. Sewall filed a criminal complaint against Adams, but the lieutenant apparently left Boston before process could be served.

In addition to providing a portent of things to come, the *Chickasaw* affair demonstrated the potential utility of invoking the writ of habeas corpus to delay or prevent the rendition of an African American alleged to be a fugitive from slavery. However, from the perspective of antislavery activists, habeas corpus had one critical drawback. Rather than having the person's status decided by a jury, all issues of law and fact were determined by a judge. A jury trial could be obtained under a different common-law writ — the writ of *de homine replegiando*, or personal replevin. Under this writ, the sheriff was required to remove the plaintiff (the alleged fugitive slave) from the defendant so that the plaintiff's status could be determined in a jury trial.

The writ of personal replevin had been used to test the status of African Americans in Massachusetts prior to the abolition of slavery in the state. Moreover, in 1787 the state legislature had guaranteed the availability of the writ to every person in the commonwealth "imprisoned, confined, or held in duress." But in 1834, commissioners appointed to revise the state statutes had averred that because habeas corpus "furnishes so complete and effectual a remedy for all cases of unlawful imprisonment or restraint . . . the writ of *de homine reple-*

giando is very seldom used." Despite this observation, the commissioners recommended retaining the action for personal replevin. Nonetheless, the legislature abolished the writ without comment as part of the general revision of the statutes in 1835.

This decision brought an immediate reaction from the antislavery forces in the state. On January 20, 1837, in response to a number of petitions requesting that those claimed as fugitives be accorded jury trials, the Judiciary Committee of the Massachusetts house of representatives was charged with the task of exploring the issue. On March 27 the committee recommended that the legislature adopt a statute reinstating the writ of personal replevin in Massachusetts.

Whig James C. Alvord prepared the report outlining the committee's reasoning. The report stressed the importance of an alleged fugitive's right to have his status determined by a jury. But at the same time, Alvord conceded that if the Fugitive Slave Act were valid, the state could not make the writ available to those claimed under the procedures established by the federal law. However, he contended that the Fugitive Slave Act was unconstitutional because the Constitution did not vest Congress with the authority to pass legislation to enforce the Fugitive Slave Clause.

In making this argument, Alvord was forced to confront the seemingly contrary authority of *Commonwealth v. Griffith*, in which the state's highest court had held that the federal statute withstood constitutional scrutiny. Alvord concluded that the legislature should not feel bound by *Griffith* for three reasons: the decision had not been unanimous, the court had not focused specifically on the federal power issue, and, in any event (at least in Alvord's view), the discussion of the constitutionality of the Fugitive Slave Act was dictum.

Against the backdrop of the Alvord report, the bill restoring the writ of personal replevin became law without fanfare in April 1837. Although cheered by abolitionists, the event seems to have passed unnoticed in the mainstream press. But events of the early 1840s would soon bring Massachusetts to the forefront in the national struggle over fugitive slaves.

Prigg v. Pennsylvania and the Fugitive Slave Act of 1850

The juxtaposition of the decision in *Griffith* and the Alvord report demonstrated that the constitutionality of the Fugitive Slave Act remained uncertain for most of the early nineteenth century. Prior to the early 1840s, the question had been addressed in a variety of different forums. The federal courts that had faced the issue had uniformly upheld the validity of the statute. However, the state courts were divided. Although the *Griffith* court was joined by the Pennsylvania Supreme Court in rejecting the constitutional challenges, a New Jersey court found the federal statute unconstitutional, and the New York courts were split.

In 1842 the Supreme Court of the United States entered the fray with its decision in *Prigg v. Pennsylvania*, the last of a trilogy of important slavery cases decided by the Court in the early 1840s. *Prigg* was a challenge to the constitutionality of Pennsylvania's revised antikidnapping statute. The evolution of that state law mirrored the development of similar statutes in a number of other Northern states. In 1820, with sectional tensions rising over the issue of slavery in Missouri and a number of prominent citizens expressing displeasure with the provision for summary proceedings in the Fugitive Slave Act, the state legislature passed a law that strengthened the protections provided to free blacks by the antikidnapping statute of 1788. The new statute stiffened the penalties for the kidnapping of free African Americans. More important, it prohibited local aldermen and justices of the peace from taking jurisdiction in cases involving runaways. Thus, the 1820 statute made it substantially more difficult for claimants to locate an official who could enforce their rights under the federal Fugitive Slave Act.

Officials in the neighboring slave state of Maryland were very disturbed by the 1820 statute. They sent commissioners to the Pennsylvania legislature to propose revisions that were far more favorable to those seeking to recover alleged fugitives. An intense political struggle ensued, and in 1826 a revised state law dealing with fugitive slaves was adopted. The new law was clearly a compromise between the demands of Maryland slaveholders and those of the antislavery forces in Pennsylvania. While abolishing the common-law right of recaption in Pennsylvania, the new law also reinstated local officials' jurisdiction over actions to recover fugitives. At the same time, the procedural requirements for the issuance of a certificate of removal by those state officials were much more stringent than those mandated by the federal law. The alleged runaway could not be detained without an affidavit from the claimant that gave a detailed description of the basis for the claim. Moreover, the oath of the owner or other interested persons would not suffice to obtain a certificate of removal, and the alleged slave was entitled to introduce evidence to refute the slave owner's claim.

Although one of the Maryland commissioners described the Pennsylvania law as "eminently useful . . . because it is a pledge that the states will adhere to the original obligations of the confederacy," other representatives of the state of Maryland were far from satisfied with the substance of the new Pennsylvania statute. Thus, it should not be surprising that the issue of fugitive slaves continued to be a source of tension between the two states. The facts of *Prigg* reflected this tension.

Prigg arose from the forcible removal of Martha Morgan from southern Pennsylvania to northern Maryland. Martha had been born late in life to a black man and woman who were enslaved to John Ashmore in Maryland. In 1812, prior to Martha's birth, her parents had been allowed to retire and continue to live on the Ashmore estate. After their retirement, Ashmore purportedly asserted on a number of occasions that he had set Martha's parents free, and he never attempted to exercise any dominion over Martha herself. Further, when Ashmore died intestate in 1824, the inventory of his estate listed two other slaves but made no mention of Martha. Nonetheless, because Ashmore had never taken the formal steps required to emancipate either Martha or her parents, Martha was clearly a slave under the laws of Maryland and thus part of the estate that passed to Ashmore's widow, Margaret.

Sometime prior to John Ashmore's death, Martha married Jerry Morgan, a free black man, and she gave birth to several children in Maryland. In 1832 they moved to York County, Pennsylvania, where she bore several more children. In February 1837 a party of four Marylanders came to Pennsylvania with the intent to return Martha to Maryland. Included in the party were Edward Prigg and Nathaniel E. Bemis, who was Margaret Ashmore's son-in-law. They obtained a warrant from Thomas Henderson, a justice of the peace in Pennsylvania, authorizing William McCreary, a constable in York County, to bring Margaret and her children before Henderson. McCreary brought the entire Morgan family, including Jerry, to Henderson's residence, but the justice determined that he lacked jurisdiction to adjudicate the matter under the relevant Pennsylvania statute.

Faced with this turn of events, the Marylanders released Jerry Morgan, telling him to return home and meet them in the morning. However, after Jerry left, Prigg, Bemis, and the remainder of their party brought Martha Morgan and the children into Maryland, where they were sold to a slave trader. Subsequently, in May 1837, Martha sued for her freedom in a Maryland county court. On August 30 a jury concluded that Martha and her children were indeed slaves owned by Margaret Ashmore. Shortly thereafter, they were sold again.

The Morgan affair caused a considerable uproar in Pennsylvania. After receiving complaints from Jerry Morgan and a number of other citizens of the state, Pennsylvania governor Joseph Ritner demanded that Maryland governor Thomas W. Veazey deliver the Marylanders to stand trial for violating Pennsylvania's antikidnapping law. Veazey initially refused, citing the fact that Prigg, Bemis, and their compatriots had not been indicted. Subsequently, an indictment was returned, and an order to arrest the men was issued. However, they were "always absent when called for."

In 1838, seeking to resolve the matter and reduce tensions with its neighbor to the north, the Maryland legislature established a commission to negotiate with the Pennsylvania state government "to make such arrangements as may be necessary to refer the questions involved to the Supreme Court of the United States, without compromising the liberty of the accused," and to secure changes in the Pennsylvania statute. Finally, on May 23, 1839, the Pennsylvania legislature passed a statute that essentially authorized a pro forma trial at which Prigg would be found guilty through a process that would ensure that the Supreme Court ultimately resolved the issues of the case.

Prigg required the justices to grapple with the complex issues raised by the Fugitive Slave Clause. Massachusetts native Joseph Story delivered the opinion of the Court. Although he had nominally been a Jeffersonian Republican at the time of his appointment, Story's basic political orientation was that of a conservative northeastern Whig. While he had taken an outspoken antislavery position in some contexts — perhaps most notably in his condemnation of the international slave trade in *The Antelope* — Story was also acutely aware of the need to reach sectional accommodations on issues such as fugitive slaves. Thus, while asserting in his *Commentaries on the Constitution of the United States* that Northern delegates to the Constitutional Convention had made a number of compromises in the face of Southern "prejudices," Story also remonstrated that

> he who wished well to his country will adhere steadily to [these compromises] as a fundamental policy which extinguishes some of the most mischievous sources of all political divisions, — those founded on geographical positions and domestic institutions. The wishes of every patriot ought now to be, *requiscat in pace*, inconsistent "with any system of law that purports to rest on the authority of reason."

Story's opinion in *Prigg* reflected an effort to balance these competing concerns. Parts of his approach had been foreshadowed in his *Commentaries on the Constitution*, where he had explicitly rejected the claim that purported fugitives were entitled to a jury trial, concluding instead that the Constitution envisioned a regime that allowed their removal based on "summary administrative procedures." Nonetheless, his opinion in *Prigg* began promisingly for the antislavery forces. It adopted the position of *Somerset v. Stewart*, the legal mainstay of the antislavery movement, and declared,

> by the general law of nations, no nation is bound to recognize the state of slavery, as to foreign slaves found within its territorial dominions, when it is in opposition to its own policy and institutions, in favor of other nations where slavery is recognized

{ *Chapter 2* }

[because] slavery is deemed to be a mere municipal regulation, founded upon and limited to the range of the territorial laws.

However, he then proceeded to outline and defend a set of conclusions that were in many cases more favorable to the pro-slavery position. Story began by arguing that the Fugitive Slave Clause was central to the creation and maintenance of the Union. Notwithstanding the fact that the provision had engendered very little discussion during the Constitutional Convention or the ratification debates, he declared that the Fugitive Slave Clause was "of the last importance to the safety and security of the southern states and could not have been surrendered by them, without endangering their whole property in slaves," that the clause "was so vital to the preservation of [the Southern states'] domestic interests and institutions that it cannot be doubted that it constituted a fundamental article without the adoption of which the Union could not have been formed," and that, in the absence of the Fugitive Slave Clause, the issue of fugitive slaves "would have created the most bitter animosities, and engendered perpetual strife between the different states." He then described the scope of the clause in sweeping terms, asserting that

> any state law or . . . regulation, which interrupts, limits, delays or postpones the right of the owner to the immediate possession of the slave, and the immediate command of his service and labor, operates, *pro tanto*, as a discharge of the slave therefrom. . . . The question is not one of quantity or degree, but of withholding or controlling the incidents of a positive and absolute right.

Story's treatment of the right of recaption followed logically from this characterization. He noted that, under the principles of the common law, the right of ownership in property carries with it the right to recover the property by self-help. He further observed that, by its terms, the Fugitive Slave Clause required even nonslave states to recognize the owner's property right in the escaped slave. Thus, Story had "not the slightest hesitation in holding, that . . . the owner of a slave is clothed with entire authority, in every state in the Union, to seize and recapture his slave, whenever he can do it, without any breach of the peace or any illegal violence."

Having embraced the pro-slavery position on recaption, Story next addressed the respective roles of the state and federal governments in enforcing the Fugitive Slave Clause. Story began this portion of the opinion by observing that government aid would often be necessary for the claimant to recover the fugitive and that the clause itself, which provides that the slave "shall be delivered up, on claim of the [putative master]," seemed to contemplate government enforcement. Against the background of this premise, he turned to the question of *which* government was charged with the duty of enforcement.

On this point, Story's argument implicitly drew on Chief Justice John Marshall's treatment of the more general concept of implied powers in *McCulloch v. Maryland*. In *Prigg*, Story relied on the basic principle that "where the end is required, the means are given; and where the duty is enjoined, the ability to perform it is contemplated to exist, on the part of the functionaries to whom it is entrusted." Thus, Story argued that since the Fugitive Slave Clause was part of the federal Constitution, "the natural inference certainly is, that the national government is clothed with the appropriate authority and functions to enforce it." He scoffed at the argument that the lack of a specific enforcement provision was fatal to this contention, declaring, "if this be the true interpretation of the constitution, it must, in a great measure, fail to attain many of its avowed objects, as a security of rights and recognition of duties," and he noted that "[Congress] has, on various occasions, exercised powers which were necessary and proper as means to carry into effect rights expressly given and duties expressly enjoined thereby." Thus, after reviewing in detail the specific provisions of the Fugitive Slave Act of 1793, he concluded that, with one specific exception, the act was "clearly constitutional, in all its leading provisions." Story thereby implicitly rejected the claim that a jury trial was required before an alleged fugitive could be seized and delivered to a claimant.

While emphasizing the power of Congress to enforce the Fugitive Slave Clause, Story downplayed the role of state governments in vindicating the claims of putative owners. Story concluded that the power to enforce the clause was vested *exclusively* in the federal government, contending that "the nature of the provision and the objects to be attained by it require that it should be controlled by one and the same will and act uniformly by the same system of regulations throughout the Union." Otherwise, he argued, the right established by the Constitution "would never, in a practical sense, be the same in all the States [but] might be enforced in some States, retarded or limited in others and denied as compulsory in many, if not in all." Thus, in Story's view, states could not pass statutes designed to vindicate the claims of owners, even if the operation of those statutes did not in any way conflict with the procedures mandated by the federal statute.

These elements of Story's opinion in *Prigg* rested almost entirely on the doctrine of federal supremacy. He did make two concessions to the principle of state autonomy, however. First, he argued that state officers could not be compelled to enforce the federal statute, although they were free to do so if required by state law. Second, he distinguished sharply between regulation of the owner's right to retake fugitive slaves and the police power of the state, concluding that under the latter authority, states retained "full jurisdiction to arrest and restrain runaway slaves, and remove them from their borders and otherwise secure themselves against their depredations and evil example."

The decision in *Prigg* brought comments from a variety of quarters. Some Southerners expressed pleasure with the decision. For example, the *Baltimore Sun* declared that *Prigg* was "all that Maryland can desire, and will be particularly agreeable to the slaveholders of the South," and the *Baltimore American* asserted that the people of Maryland would view the decision as a "triumphant vindication of their rights." Conversely, some antislavery Northerners were displeased by the decision. Thus, the *New York Daily Express* complained that "the conclusion to which the Court have arrived involves consequences which can by no means be satisfactory to this part of the country," and the *New York Tribune* declared, "there is not a man in the Free states . . . whose personal liberty is not invaded and endangered by [the decision]." Similarly, in February 1843 a joint committee of the Massachusetts legislature declared that Story's opinion "assumes as a rule of practical value, that slavery must . . . be sustained even at the cost of all the safeguards of liberty," and it concluded that "a decision which arrives at a result so shocking to the feelings and the principles of every citizen in a land of freedom, must be in its principle erroneous."

But some Northerners took a less jaundiced view of *Prigg*. They recognized that those seeking to recover fugitive slaves might have to rely on the aid of state and local officials and that Story had clearly left the states free to refuse such aid. For example, while complaining that the decision unduly concentrated authority in the federal government, the *Ohio Observer* also noted, "it is the opinion of many that, by this decision, the fugitive slave will be *in fact*, more secure in any free State, since, by it, all State officers are exempted . . . from having any thing to do, one way or the other with him." It was this aspect of *Prigg* that would soon take center stage in Massachusetts.

The occasion was the aftermath of an effort by James B. Gray, a slave owner from Norfolk, Virginia, to lay claim to the ownership of George Latimer, an African American who had recently arrived in Boston from Norfolk. Gray not only claimed that Latimer was a slave who had escaped from his service; he also came to Boston armed with the charge that Latimer had committed larceny while in Norfolk. On October 19, 1842, a warrant for Latimer's arrest on the larceny charge was served on him by one Constable Stratton, who, acting as Gray's agent, transported Latimer to the local jail.

Acting on Latimer's behalf, antislavery attorneys Samuel Eliot Sewall and Amos Merrill immediately petitioned Massachusetts chief justice Lemuel Shaw for a writ of habeas corpus. On October 20 a hearing was held before the entire Supreme Judicial Court. After a number of witnesses testified that Latimer was in fact enslaved to Gray, Shaw ordered Latimer to be remanded to the custody of Stratton. Shaw reasoned that, under the terms of the Fugitive Slave Act and Story's opinion in *Prigg*, Gray had the right to detain Latimer for a reasonable time in order to bring the putative slave before a federal tribunal for the purpose of obtaining a certificate of removal. Given that Gray had testified that he intended to take such actions immediately, Shaw found no legal justification for requiring that Latimer be removed from Stratton's custody. Thus, Latimer was returned to his jail cell, but only after Stratton and his assistants repulsed a violent mob effort to free Latimer.

The following day, after agreeing to postpone consideration of the larceny complaint upon the posting of $200 bail, Gray petitioned Justice Story for the necessary certificate of removal. Over the protests of Latimer's attorneys, Story postponed the hearing for two weeks to give Gray an opportunity to retrieve the documents demonstrating his title from Norfolk. In the interim, Story ordered that Latimer remain in Gray's custody, with the proviso that Latimer not be removed from Massachusetts and that his attorneys have access to him at "reasonable times" until the hearing was held. Amid great public outcry, Latimer was once again returned to jail, now in the custody of jailer Nathaniel Coolidge.

On October 24 Latimer's supporters made a final effort to obtain legal redress for him under Massachusetts law. Invoking the provisions of the Personal Liberty Law of 1837 in the Court of Common Pleas, they offered a $1,000 bond and obtained a writ of personal replevin that required Coolidge to produce Latimer for a jury trial on his claim of freedom. Coolidge refused to acknowledge the writ, and Sewall and Merrill petitioned Chief Justice Shaw to order Coolidge to comply. Shaw, however, refused to order Latimer released, declaring that "an appeal to natural rights and the paramount law of liberty was not pertinent" and that Shaw was forbidden by the Constitution and the Fugitive Slave Act to interfere in the case.

Despite their legal setbacks, abolitionists and their allies continued to press for Latimer's release. At a mass meeting held at Faneuil Hall on October 30, speakers attacked not only the Fugitive Slave Clause but also the Constitution as a whole, and they labeled Story "slave-catcher-in-chief for the New England States." In addition, they condemned Coolidge for continuing to allow Gray to house Latimer at the jail, noting that state law mandated the use of public facilities only for "persons detained or committed by the authority of the Courts of the United States, as well as the courts and magistrates of this commonwealth." They observed that Story's order had simply remanded Latimer to Gray's custody; it did not require that the putative slave be held in jail pending resumption of the hearing.

Ultimately, it was the latter point that proved decisive. When the hearing on the request for a certificate of removal reconvened on November 5, Story was ill. In his place sat Peleg Sprague, the district judge for Massachusetts. Gray was ready to proceed; however, Latimer's attorneys requested a postponement until November 21 so that they could obtain testimony from witnesses in Norfolk who would support Latimer's contention that he had been freed by the terms of a previous master's will that had been destroyed without being probated. Sprague granted the second postponement, and on November 17 the local sheriff ordered Coolidge to release Latimer before noon on November 18. At that point, fearing that a riot would deprive him of his possession in any event, Gray agreed to release his claim under the Fugitive Slave Act for $400 — far less than he had spent in his effort to reclaim Latimer. Subsequently, the governor of Virginia sought to have Latimer extradited on the larceny charge, but Governor John Davis of Massachusetts refused to honor the request.

Reactions to the resolution of the dispute split along predictable lines. Southerners and their allies were outraged. The *Niles Register* reported that the Latimer affair had created the "utmost indignation" in Virginia and was viewed as "a violation of the compact under which we are confederated." The *Norfolk Herald* declared that "[Gray] has been defrauded of his property by a mockery of justice and forms of law twisted and contrived to defeat all his efforts to obtain his just rights." The *New York Union* described the Latimer affair as "the boldest and most open violation of the Constitution by the abolitionists that we have yet on record." The mayor of Norfolk called a mass meeting "to take into consideration the outrageous proceedings of the Abolitionists, High Sheriff and other authorities of Boston." A committee appointed at that meeting condemned what it described as "a want of fidelity to the high and solemn behest of [the Constitution]" and called on Congress to adopt a more effective statutory remedy for those seeking to recover fugitive slaves.

The antislavery forces, in contrast, were exultant. Though suggesting that those participating in the sale of Latimer had violated state law against slave trading, the *Boston Courier* nonetheless celebrated "a victory of principle . . . gained for the free men of the North . . . over the arbitrary slave-holding policy of the South." Similarly, the *Emancipator and Free American* declared that Massachusetts "has gained a most glorious yet bloodless victory."

In the wake of this denouement, the protectors of fugitive slaves also realized that Story had left them with a powerful weapon to use against slave hunters: his conclusion that state officials could not be compelled to cooperate in efforts to recover escaped slaves. The ultimate failure of James B. Gray's mission demonstrated that only strong government action could vindicate the strictures of the Fugitive Slave Clause and its implementing statute in the face of an aroused public opposition. Moreover, during the Jacksonian era, the vast majority of government resources belonged to the states rather than the federal government. Slave owners who were denied access to these resources would have a far more difficult time recapturing those who had escaped from bondage.

Against this background, the antislavery forces in Massachusetts quickly amassed more than 60,000 signatures on petitions urging the legislature to pass a statute denying all state government aid to slave owners seeking to recover fugitive slaves. The petitions were referred to a joint committee of the Massachusetts legislature, which in February 1843 issued a report excoriating *Prigg* and calling for the passage of such a statute. In response, by near-unanimous votes, both houses of the Massachusetts legislature passed a new personal liberty law on March 23, and Governor Marcus Morton signed the law the next day. The new law prohibited all judicial officials from taking jurisdiction over any claim that arose under the Fugitive Slave Act. In addition, the statute prohibited state officials from "arresting, detaining, or aiding in the arrest or detention" of alleged fugitives from service or from detaining such fugitives in any public building in the state.

Subsequent events provided additional fuel for Southern anger. The actions of the Massachusetts legislature proved to be a model for other Northern states, leading to a new round of personal liberty laws. By 1848, those seeking to recover fugitive slaves were also unable to call on state officials for aid in Connecticut, Ohio, Pennsylvania, Rhode Island, and Vermont. At times, antislavery Northerners went even further, mobilizing direct resistance to slave owners' efforts to reclaim fugitives. In one particularly well-publicized occurrence, the so-called McKlintock Riot of 1847, James Kennedy, a Maryland slave owner, was killed when a group of Carlisle, Pennsylvania, residents tried to prevent him and a companion from returning to Maryland with three fugitives who had escaped to Carlisle.

Southerners viewed such incidents as evidence of Northerners' disdain for the constitutional obligations owed to slave owners. For example, a Virginia legislative committee characterized the new round of personal liberty laws as a "disgusting and revolting exhibition of faithless and unconstitutional legislation" designed to perpetrate "palpable frauds upon the South, calculated to excite at once her indignation and her contempt." Similarly, in 1849 John C. Calhoun complained that "the attempt to recover a slave, in most of the Northern States, cannot now be made without the hazard of insult, heavy pecuniary loss, imprisonment, and even of life itself," and in 1850 an unidentified Southern commentator would assert that "no decision of the Supreme Court has produced more evil consequences than [*Prigg*]. It has embarrassed the owners of slaves in recovering their property in the free states. It has encouraged the abolitionists in their efforts to increase those embarrassments." In isolation, such expressions of dissatisfaction would have been insufficient to induce a Northern-dominated House of Representatives to adopt a strengthened Fugitive Slave Act. However, in 1850 the renewed dispute over the issue of slavery in the territories created a political climate in which the passage of such a statute was possible.

The spark that ignited the controversy that ultimately led to passage of the Fugitive Slave Act of 1850 was the petition of the people of California for admission as a free state. This petition set off an intense debate in Congress, which split along sectional lines and included not only discussions of California but also a general discussion about the fate of slavery in the totality of the Mexican cession, as well as the boundaries of the recently acquired slave state of Texas. With secession looming as a real possibility, an overhaul of the Fugitive Slave Act became an important part of the compromise package that resolved the crisis.

Efforts to obtain new legislation on fugitive slaves in the 31st Congress actually began independently of discussions of the territorial issue. The bill initially drafted by Democratic senator James Mason of Virginia and reported by the Senate Judiciary Committee on January 16, 1850, would have greatly expanded the number of federal officials empowered to issue certificates of removal. Whereas the 1793 statute gave this power only to federal judges and state officials, the Mason bill provided that a certificate of removal could be issued by "any commissioner, or clerk of [the district] courts, or marshal thereof, or any postmaster . . . or collector of customs." The Mason bill also doubled the fine imposed on those who aided fugitive slaves.

On January 28 Whig senator William Seward of New York responded by introducing a bill that would have provided for jury trials for alleged fugitive slaves, required judges to grant writs of habeas corpus for alleged fugitives who were seized, and imposed stiff penalties on judges who refused to issue such writs. Just as they had prior to 1850, antislavery Northerners argued that the provision of jury trials was nothing more than an application of ordinary principles of fairness. Thus, for example, Free-Soil senator John P. Hale of New Hampshire asserted, "I would never consent to purchase peace by the surrender of such a valuable right, as that valuable right, 'formidable,' in the words of the Declaration of Independence, 'to tyrants only.'" Such sentiments were widespread in the North. Thus, despite his famous declaration that, on the issue of fugitive slaves, "the South is right, and the North is wrong," even Daniel Webster ultimately introduced a bill requiring jury trials.

Not surprisingly, Southerners had a quite different perspective. For example, viewing the Seward bill as a device to prevent slave owners from exercising their legitimate right to retake fugitives, Democratic senator Henry S. Foote bitterly argued that the bill "was designed to cap the climax of southern wrongs, to cause the oppression at once to overflow, and to force us of the South . . . to secede from the Union, or, remaining in it, to submit to a wanton, heartless and insulting deprivation of all our constitutional rights, such as no free people has ever been known patiently to endure." The proposal on fugitive slaves that emerged from the compromise Committee of Thirteen clearly reflected this view as well.

On May 8 Henry Clay presented the committee's proposals to the full Senate. Clay began by embracing the basic Southern position on fugitive slaves. He first analogized the delivery of escaped slaves to the extradition of fugitives from justice, observing that "the procedure uniformly is summary. It has never been thought necessary to apply, in cases of that kind, the forms and ceremony of a final trial." He also dismissed the possibility that jury trials were necessary to ensure that free blacks would not be kidnapped into slavery under the pretense of being fugitives, noting that "if there have been any instances of abuse in the erroneous arrests of fugitives from service or labor, the committee have not obtained knowledge of them" and "believe that none such have occurred, and are not likely to occur." Clay further contended that if a jury trial were required in the state where the alleged fugitive was found, "under the name of a popular and cherished institution . . . there would be a complete mockery of justice, so far as the owner of the fugitive is concerned." He asserted that even if a jury ruled in favor of the claimant, "[the claimant] would have to bear all the burden and expense of the litigation, without indemnity, and would learn by sad experience, that he had by far better abandoned his right in the first instance, than to establish it at such unremunerated cost and heavy sacrifice." Finally, Clay noted that all the Southern states provided that the alleged fugitive would have a forum to pursue a claim for freedom after he had been returned.

Despite his embrace of the basic Southern perspective, Clay offered two amendments to the Mason bill as concessions to Northern opinion. The first would have required the claimant to carry with him, "when practicable," a record, obtained in an ex parte proceeding before a court of his home state, describing the alleged fugitive and the facts surrounding his escape. Second, in cases in which the person seized denied that he was an escaped slave, the claimant would have been required to post a bond in the state where the alleged fugitive was found, pending a full trial before a tribunal in the claimant's state; at such a trial, the seized African American would be entitled to introduce evidence rebutting the claimant's assertion that he was in fact an escaped slave. By having these amendments adopted, Clay hoped to allay Northern concerns about the potential kidnapping of free blacks, while maintaining Southern control over the rendition process.

Clay's proposals were acceptable to neither side. Democratic senator Pierre Soule of Louisiana observed that the proposals did nothing to obviate the costs to slave owners associated with full jury trials and claimed that they were tantamount to the assertion of federal control over the state institution of slavery. Conversely, arguing for jury trials in the states where the alleged fugitives were found, Whig senator William L. Dayton of New Jersey complained that the Clay proposals reduced Northern officials to "the mere executive, the mere ministerial officers of the slave States, for the purpose of carrying their judgments into effect." Against this background, the compromise proposals were rejected without even a recorded vote on August 19.

Mason then brought forward a revised version of the bill he had introduced earlier in the session. Northern Whigs continued to press for a jury trial requirement, but their proposals were easily defeated. An amendment by Whig senator Thomas Pratt of Maryland that would have required the U.S. government to compensate owners for fugitives who were not delivered met a similar fate on August 22. Pratt was opposed unanimously by Northerners and by many Southerners as well; some of them objected in principle to the extension of any federal authority over slavery, and others suggested that the proposal amounted to a compensated emancipation scheme. On August 23 Mason's bill passed the Senate by a vote of 27–10, with three Northern Democrats joining a united South. On September 12 the House of Representatives followed suit by a vote of 109–76, as Northern Democrats provided the margin of victory for the bill. With the territorial issue having been settled on relatively favorable terms for the North, many Northerners in both houses simply chose to abstain.

The Fugitive Slave Act of 1850 provided for the appointment of a greatly expanded number of federal officials empowered to act as commissioners for the purpose of issuing certificates of removal and also charged these officials with the duty of hearing claims of putative masters "in a summary manner." Upon receiving "satisfactory proof" of the validity of the claimant's assertion of ownership—defined as either a sworn statement taken by the responsible official himself or a document certifying that appropriate testimony had been given before an official in the state from which the alleged escape had occurred—the federal commissioner was to issue a certificate for removal of the alleged fugitive. The testimony of the alleged runaway himself was explicitly deemed inadmissible. The commissioner was to be paid $10 per case if he found for the claimant, but $5 if he found against the claimant.

Once a certificate of removal was issued, no court was allowed to interfere with the removal of the alleged fugitive. The claimant was entitled to enlist the aid of federal marshals in securing and returning the alleged fugitive to his home state, and the marshals were liable for the full value of any fugitive who escaped. Moreover, the commissioners were empowered to summon ordinary citizens to act as a *posse comitatus* to apprehend the alleged fugitive. Finally, the statute increased the penalties for those who interfered with the apprehension of alleged fugitives.

The passage of the 1850 statute set the stage for a new round of disputes over the rendition of fugitive slaves. Once again, Boston would emerge as a flash point in the conflict.

CHAPTER 3

Massachusetts Responds

For many Southerners, enforcement of the Fugitive Slave Act of 1850 was the linchpin of the entire compromise package. Thus, a convention called in the state of Georgia adopted a platform declaring that Georgia "does not wholly approve [of the act but] will abide by it as a permanent adjustment of this sectional controversy"; the same convention also proclaimed that "it is the deliberate opinion of this Convention, that upon the faithful execution of the Fugitive Slave Bill by the proper authorities depends the preservation of our much loved Union." Making the same point more bluntly, a North Carolina newspaper editor warned the free states to "respect and enforce the Fugitive Slave Law as it stands. If not, WE WILL LEAVE YOU."

Northerners were split. The intensity of the division was nowhere more apparent than in the city of Boston. Many Bostonians were outraged by the statute. For example, the *Boston Pathfinder* asserted that the Fugitive Slave Act was "better suited to the climate of Russia than to the free atmosphere of democratic America, if it be not a misnomer to call a nation free or democratic, with such laws on its statute-book," and the more conservative *Boston Daily Atlas* proclaimed that "words are almost inadequate to express our mortification and disappointment at [the passage of the act]." However, because of their unionist sentiments and close ties to Southern elites, other members of Boston's social and political establishment voiced support for the new statute.

The most prominent standard-bearer of this group was Daniel Webster, one of the foremost Whig political leaders of the Jacksonian era. For much of his career, Webster had been a champion of the antislavery cause, opposing the extension of slavery to Missouri, leading the fight against the gag rule in the Senate, and at one point premising a bid for the presidency on his opposition to the acquisition of Texas. But Webster was also a staunch unionist, and it was this aspect of his political philosophy that came to the fore during the crisis of 1850. In what became known as the Seventh of March speech in the Senate, he pleaded for compromise, famously declaring that, on the subject of fugitive slaves, "the South is right, and the North is wrong."

By the time the Fugitive Slave Act of 1850 became law, Webster had resigned from the Senate to enter Millard Fillmore's cabinet as secretary of state. In that capacity, Webster pressed hard for enforcement of the new statute. He not only approved of the compromise measures in principle but also hoped to use his support for the compromise as the centerpiece of an effort to achieve his lifelong ambition – gaining the presidency – in 1852.

Webster and his allies were opposed by a biracial coalition of outright abolitionists, antislavery Whigs, antislavery Democrats, and members of the Free-Soil Party, which had been formed in 1848 in the wake of the dispute over the Wilmot Proviso. At a mass meeting held on October 14 at Faneuil Hall, leaders of this coalition excoriated the Fugitive Slave Act and called on the public to resist its enforcement. For example, Charles Francis Adams declared that the statute "fills us all with mingled sensations of astonishment and horror" and that "no imperial edict of Rome's worst days was ever marked with a more burning stamp of human passion than this bill." Similarly, the Reverend Nathaniel Colver called for a resolution that provided that, "Constitution or no Constitution, law or no law, we will not allow a fugitive slave to be taken from Massachusetts." The meeting also selected fifty men to serve on a Vigilance Committee, which was charged with the task of "tak[ing] all measures which they shall deem expedient to protect the colored people of this city in the enjoyment of their lives and liberties." In addition, an executive committee of eight men was appointed to help organize the defense of fugitive slaves on an ongoing basis under the leadership of the Reverend Theodore Parker, a fiery abolitionist.

The committee members did not have to wait long before their services were required. On Saturday, October 19, Willis H. Hughes, the jailer of Macon, Georgia, arrived in Boston with two companions. Acting on behalf of fellow Georgian Robert Collins, his mission was to capture William and Ellen Craft, a married couple who had been enslaved to Collins before escaping in 1848. The Crafts were among the best-known fugitive slaves in the country. After their escape they had revealed their identities in Philadelphia and had given lectures to antislavery groups in both the United States and England. Eventually they settled in Boston, where William opened a furniture-making and repair business and Ellen worked as a seamstress.

On October 21 Hughes began his efforts to reclaim the Crafts by applying for warrants for their arrest from Justice Levi Woodbury, the circuit justice for Massachusetts. Woodbury stated that he was not the official responsible for issuing such warrants and recommended that Hughes consult George Lunt, the U.S. district attorney. Lunt expressed great reluctance to handle fugitive slave cases and directed Hughes to Democrat Benjamin Hallett, a commissioner of the federal district court. Hallett incorrectly informed Hughes that it was the duty of the claimant to arrest the alleged fugitive without government assistance and then bring the putative slave before a commissioner for a determination of whether a certificate of removal should be issued. When Hughes persisted, Hallett told him to come back the next morning, at which time Hallett informed Hughes that if he filled out a legal form, Hallett would consider the application for the arrest warrants.

At this point, Hughes came to the conclusion that he required professional legal counsel and retained Seth J. Thomas, a friend of Webster. Thomas first applied for the warrants from Peleg Sprague, who equivocated. Thomas then turned to George Ticknor Curtis, another commissioner of the local federal district court. After Curtis had met with Woodbury, Sprague, and his fellow commissioners, it was agreed that Hughes should plead his case before Woodbury and Sprague in their chambers the following morning. At that time, Hughes was informed that he would have to seek the arrest warrants in open court. After following this procedure, Hughes finally received the warrants on the morning of Friday, October 25.

When the warrants were issued, the antislavery community in Boston mobilized its forces in defense of the Crafts. Crowds gathered to monitor the activities of Charles Devens, the U.S. marshal charged with serving the warrants on the Crafts. To harass Hughes, lawyers for the Vigilance Committee filed a series of criminal complaints against him and had him arrested for slandering William Craft and injuring Craft's business by describing him as a slave, carrying concealed weapons, and smoking and swearing in the street. In each case, Hughes was forced to post a large bond to retain his freedom. Chanting, hostile crowds also followed Hughes and his companions wherever they went in the city.

Antislavery lawyers also warned Devens that they would bring legal proceedings against him if he exceeded his legal authority in even the slightest degree. Faced with this threat, Devens showed little enthusiasm for serving the warrants. At one point, he declined to serve the warrants because of conflicting information about the Crafts' whereabouts. On another occasion, after William Craft barricaded himself in his carpentry shop and refused him entrance, Devens — fearing that he had no legal authority to break through the door to serve the warrants — departed without making any effort to do so. After an investigation, Attorney General John J. Crittenden later concluded that Devens was not guilty of dereliction of duty; however, Crittenden also observed, "I can see no evidence of any activity or energy on [Devens's] part" and that "a more commendable activity and energy might have been exerted by [him]."

Against this background, on Wednesday, October 30, the Reverend Parker and a delegation from the Vigilance Committee went to Hughes's hotel room and warned him that he and his companions "were not safe in Boston another night." With his mission to reclaim the Crafts apparently stalemated, Hughes left Boston the following day. Although Hughes vowed to return and complete his task, in early November the Vigilance Committee spirited the Crafts away, taking them first to Portland, Maine, and then to Nova Scotia. From there they sailed to England, where they lived out their lives as celebrities.

Not surprisingly, Southerners were not pleased with this outcome. For example, the *Mississippi Free Trader and Natchez Gazette* decried what it described as "Yankee Nullification" and observed that "this is the way . . . that laws are set at defiance in Boston and the Constitution of the country trampled under foot." The *Macon Journal and Messenger* decried what it characterized as the "bad faith" of both Devens and Curtis in delaying the rendition proceedings and thereby allowing the Vigilance Committee to effectively mobilize opposition to the recapture of the Crafts.

Fillmore, Webster, and their supporters were similarly angered and frustrated by the success of the anticompromise forces in defeating the effort to reclaim the Crafts. On November 9 Fillmore sent a letter to Robert Collins apologizing for the failure to secure the Crafts and promising that, in the future, all necessary force would be used to carry out the provisions of the Fugitive Slave Act to the letter. In Boston, the Websterites held a mass Union meeting in Faneuil Hall on November 26. At the meeting a number of resolutions were passed supporting the Compromise of 1850, and a variety of speakers emphasized the need to prevent agitation over slavery from disrupting the Union. The most widely noted speech was that of Benjamin Robbins Curtis, the brother of George Ticknor Curtis and one of the most eminent lawyers in Boston. Curtis would later become famous for his dissent from the Supreme Court's pro-slavery decision in the *Dred Scott* case; however, in the early 1850s the Curtis family (who would become known collectively as the "Curtii") was closely identified with Daniel Webster and his policy of seeking accommodation with the slave states. Indeed, even before the November 26 meeting, at the request of the U.S. marshal's office, Curtis had provided a legal opinion vindicating the constitutionality of the Fugitive Slave Act of 1850. Thus, he was the ideal candidate to deliver a comprehensive Websterite response to the furor that erupted in Boston with the passage of the Fugitive Slave Act of 1850 and the unsuccessful effort to capture the Crafts.

Curtis's argument rested on three major contentions. First, he emphasized the fact that the Fugitive Slave Clause was an integral part of the Constitution and that the citizens of Massachusetts were bound to respect both the state's 1789 decision to adhere to the new structure of government and the forms of law more generally. Thus, although Curtis observed that "so far as [God] has supplied us with the means to succor the distressed, we, as Christian men, will do so, and bid them welcome," he also averred that "we will not violate a solemn compact to do it; we will not do it by holding up our hand and swearing to render a verdict according to the law and the evidence, and then knowingly violate that oath; we will not plunge into civil discord to do it; [and] we will not shed blood to do it."

Second, Curtis emphasized the need to seek accommodation with the slave states — a need that he viewed as deriving as much from geography as from the existence of the Union:

Without an obligation to restore fugitives from service, Constitution or no Constitution, we could not expect to live in peace with the slave-holding states. . . . You may break up the Constitution and the Union to-morrow . . . you may do it in any conceivable or inconceivable way; you may draw the geographical line between slave-holding and non-slave-holding *anywhere*; but when we have settled down, they will have their institutions and we shall have ours. One is as much a fact as the other. One engages the interests and feelings and passions of men as much as the other. And how long can we live in peace, side by side, without some provision by compact, to meet this case? Not one year.

Finally, Curtis argued that, even in the abstract, Massachusetts owed no obligation to escaped slaves:

With the rights of [fugitive slaves] I firmly believe Massachusetts has nothing to do. It is enough for us that they have no right to be *here*. Our peace and safety they have no right to invade; whether they come as fugitives, and being here, act as rebels against our law, or whether they come as armed invaders. Whatever natural rights they have, and I admit those natural rights to their fullest extent, *this* is not the *soil* on which to vindicate them.

Not surprisingly, Curtis's speech was not well received by the opponents of the Fugitive Slave Act. While conceding that the speech was "very able," a correspondent for the *New York Independent* also averred that "the overwhelming majority of the people of Massachusetts loathe [the fugitive slave] law, and their good sense is not [to] be put down by the sneers and denunciations even of so (ordinarily) excellent a man as Mr. B. R. Curtis." The *Boston Republican* was less temperate, describing the oration as "one of the most cold-blooded, heartless and infamous speeches that ever fell from the lips of men" and asserting that the speech "shows him to be a narrow, bigoted and heartless demagogue, ready to pander to the prejudices, and lowest and basest sentiments of the meanest portion of our population." With the battle lines thus drawn, the next major skirmish in the campaign came in February 1851 over the effort to recapture Shadrach

Minkins. In early May 1850 Minkins had escaped to Boston by sea from Norfolk, where he had been enslaved to John DeBree. Minkins worked as a waiter until Wednesday, February 12, 1851, when John Caphart, a constable from Norfolk, arrived in Boston with legal authorization from DeBree to secure Minkins's recapture. Caphart quickly and quietly obtained an arrest warrant from Commissioner George Ticknor Curtis, and on Friday, February 14, the warrant was conveyed to the marshal's office for execution.

Charles Devens had been called to Washington to explain his actions in the Craft affair, so the task of executing the warrant on Minkins fell to Assistant Deputy Marshal Patrick Riley. On February 15 Riley and his men seized Minkins at his place of employment. Because the Massachusetts personal liberty law forbade the use of the city jail to detain putative fugitive slaves, Minkins was brought to the federal courthouse for incarceration. With memories of the Craft debacle fresh in his mind, Riley posted guards at the main entrance to the courthouse and ordered all other doors closed.

News of the arrest spread quickly, and a crowd of more than 150 people soon gathered at the courthouse. In addition, the Vigilance Committee assembled a group of seven lawyers to orchestrate Minkins's defense. Richard Henry Dana and Robert Morris, the first African American admitted to the Massachusetts bar, prepared a petition for a writ of habeas corpus, and Dana sought out Chief Justice Shaw in the state courthouse and presented him with the petition. Shaw wanted no part of the controversy; after sparring with Dana over a number of technicalities, the chief justice finally stated that the writ could not be issued because allegations in the petition itself showed that Minkins was in the legal custody of a U.S. marshal.

At almost the same time, Seth Thomas, representing Caphart, was arguing for a certificate of removal in a crowded courtroom over which Commissioner George Ticknor Curtis presided. Noting that the documentation clearly established DeBree's ownership, Thomas pressed for a speedy resolution of the case, arguing that "there is nothing in the case but a question of identity." But Samuel Sewall, observing that he and the other lawyers for Minkins had become aware of the case only fifteen minutes before, moved for a postponement, and Curtis adjourned the proceedings for three days, until 10 AM on Tuesday, February 18.

Minkins was almost certain to be returned to slavery when the hearing was reconvened, but other events intervened. Initially, Riley and his men were successful in clearing the courtroom following the postponement. However, at 2 PM, as the door to the courtroom was opened to allow Charles G. Davis, the last of Minkins's attorneys, to leave, the crowd stormed the door and forcibly removed Minkins from the custody of the federal marshals. Minkins was then brought to a private home in Boston, where he stayed until he was transported by taxicab to the Cambridge home of the Reverend Joseph C. Lovejoy, brother of abolitionist martyr Elijah Lovejoy, who had been murdered by an antiabolitionist mob in Alton, Illinois, in 1837. Ultimately, Minkins found his way to Montreal, where he lived without incident until his death on December 13, 1875.

Once again, reactions to the rescue of Shadrach Minkins broke along predictable lines. Abolitionists and others who were strongly opposed to enforcement of the Fugitive Slave Act were exultant. The Reverend Henry Bowditch, a member of the Vigilance Committee, asserted, "I think [the rescue] is the most noble deed done in Boston since the destruction of the tea in 1773." Similarly, upon hearing news of the rescue, Henry C. Wright of Ohio declared himself "wild with joy." Conversely, Southerners and pro-compromise Northerners were outraged. The *Savannah Republican* described the city of Boston as "a black speck on the map, disgraced by the lowest, the meanest, the BLACKEST kind of NULLIFICATION." The *Boston Daily Times* condemned the rescue as "one of the most lawless and atrocious acts that has ever blackened the character of any community," and the *New York Herald* proclaimed, "if we are not mistaken, this is the greatest outrage that ever occurred in the United States."

The U.S. Senate soon joined the fray. On February 18, expressing his indignation at the "outrage" of the Minkins rescue, Senator Henry Clay of Kentucky offered a resolution that called on President Fillmore to inform the Senate of the measures he intended to take in response to the rescue. Clay focused on the fact that the crowd that had freed Minkins had been composed primarily of African Americans, a group that Clay described as "people who possess no part . . . in our political system." He thundered that "the question which arises is, whether we shall have law, and whether the majesty of the Government shall be maintained or not; whether we shall have Government of white men or black men in the cities of this country."

Even Whig senator John Davis of Massachusetts and Free-Soil senator John P. Hale of New Hampshire joined Clay in noting their disapproval of the Minkins rescue, albeit in much milder tones. But Davis coupled his expression of disapproval with the observation that the Fugitive Slave Act itself was "offensive," and Hale pointedly analogized the actions of the rescuers to those of violent antiabolitionist protesters in Kentucky. Moreover, while Davis averred that the vast majority of Massachusetts residents would obey the commands of the Fugitive Slave Act if the statute's constitutionality was vindicated by the courts, Hale warned against any effort to use the military to enforce the law and observed that "if the moral sentiment of the people among whom the laws are to be enforced is not sufficient to enforce them, they cannot be enforced."

On the latter point, Hale found a somewhat unlikely ally in Democratic senator Jefferson Davis of Mississippi. Though noting that he had been a strong supporter of the Fugitive Slave Act in 1850, Davis observed, "I feared then, what seems to be too well realized now, that there was not a sentiment in the northern states to enforce the law, and without that public sentiment, without that consent . . . the law was useless." Davis linked the Minkins rescue to the inaction of government officials in the Craft affair, which he characterized as "a direct encouragement to a free negro mob to set aside the law, and to oppose the officers if they attempted to execute it." But at the same time, he declared that "it would be a total subversion of the principles of our government if the strong arm of the United States is to be brought to crush the known will of the people of any state of this Union," and he invited the citizens of Massachusetts to secede from the Union if they found the demands of the Fugitive Slave Act to be intolerable.

Though it called for restraint from the Fillmore administration, Davis's speech, like that of Clay before him, also reflected rising Southern anger over what many in the slave states viewed as the Northern states' refusal to fulfill their obligations to their Southern compatriots. Against this background, Fillmore, Webster, and their allies were determined to demonstrate that the federal government would not tolerate Northern intransigence. Even before the Senate discussions, the secretaries of war and the navy had issued orders that made federal military forces available to the local federal marshal if he certified that he was confronted with forces "too powerful to be overcome by the civil authority." On February 19 Fillmore issued a proclamation that called on the citizenry of Boston to obey the laws and called for civil and military authorities to take whatever actions were necessary to prevent further civil unrest and to help capture Minkins. In addition, the proclamation specifically directed that "prosecutions be commenced against all persons who have made themselves aides or abettors in this flagitious offense," and on February 20 Webster characterized the actions of the rescuers as "nothing less than treason."

The Boston city government expressed analogous sentiments. On February 18 the Board of Mayor and Aldermen passed a resolution expressing regret that the city's dignity had been criminally insulted and instructing the city marshal to deploy "the whole police force," if necessary, to prevent further slave rescues. Two days later the Common Council endorsed both this course of action and Fillmore's proclamation.

The prosecutions called for by Fillmore had in fact been initiated even before the presidential proclamation was issued. On February 17 both Elizur Wright and Charles G. Davis were arrested and charged with giving the signal to attack the courthouse. Soon thereafter, Robert Morris, Lewis Hayden, and eight other African American men were also arrested and charged with helping to plan the rescue and participating in its execution. After a preliminary hearing, Commissioner Benjamin Hallett — a staunch supporter of the Compromise of 1850 — concluded on February 26 that the charges against Davis should be dismissed. However, before the other defendants could be tried, a variety of other events intervened.

First, to some state legislators, the Shadrach Minkins affair pointed to a need to strengthen the Massachusetts personal liberty law. Shortly after Minkins's escape, a Joint Special Committee that had been impaneled to deal with issues related to slavery solicited Richard Henry Dana and Charles Sumner to help draft a new personal liberty law "to meet the dangers and outrages of the Fugitive Slave Bill." In late March the committee reported the bill that Dana and Sumner had crafted.

The committee proposal was accompanied by a report prepared by Whig senator Joseph T. Buckingham. Much of the report was devoted to a harsh attack on the institution of slavery in general. Buckingham arraigned slavery as "utterly inconsistent with the natural law of God, with the general design of all just human laws . . . with the special design of the Constitution as set forth in the Preamble . . . and . . . with the express words of the Declaration of Independence." The report conceded that citizens owed "obligations" to the Constitution and "allegiance to their country and the government which it has established." But at the same time, Buckingham stopped short of positing a duty to obey constitutional provisions that sustained slavery, stating only that "*if* [the] provisions sustaining slavery be complied with . . . it should be distinctly stated that compliance is rendered not because it is *morally right*, but because it is *technically legal*; nay, technically legal while it was absolutely wrong, and contrary to the avowed design of the Constitution."

Turning to the issue of fugitive slaves particularly, Buckingham blasted the Fugitive Slave Act as "morally — not legally but morally — invalid and void" and compared those who sought to recover escaped slaves to participants in the African slave trade. In addition, deploying a number of standard antislavery critiques, the report characterized the statute as "unconstitutional, not merely technically and in its details, but [also] unconstitutional universally and in the highest degree, as tending to defeat the purposes of the Constitution itself." Finally, Buckingham noted that the *Prigg* Court had explicitly vindicated the right of the states to refuse to allow their instrumentalities to be used in the enforcement of the Fugitive Slave Act of 1793.

This observation provided the backdrop for the bill the committee introduced. Recognizing that the Personal Liberty Law of 1843 had referred specifically to the Fugitive Slave Act of 1793 in prohibiting judges and other law enforcement officials from participating in the rendition of fugitive slaves, the 1851 bill explicitly barred the same officials from aiding in the enforcement of the 1850 federal statute. It also extended the prohibition to members of the volunteer militia who might be called on by the U.S. marshal to keep order during rendition proceedings. In addition, the new bill required local district attorneys to come to the defense of those claimed as fugitives and explicitly provided that state courts should issue writs of habeas corpus in fugitive slave cases. Finally, the bill provided that anyone claimed as a fugitive could bring an action against the claimant in state court, and the claimant would be subject to fine or imprisonment unless he could prove "by evidence" that the person being claimed was in fact a fugitive.

The committee proposal drew heated denunciations from much of the mainstream press in Massachusetts. The *Boston Traveller*, for example, declared that the bill was "certainly one of the most extraordinary ever reported in Massachusetts. It breathes the spirit of open nullification." It continued by observing that "the passage of such a law as this . . . would place [Massachusetts] on a par with South Carolina; it would make the tail of that monster of which South Carolina is the head — Nullification." The *Springfield Republican* expressed similar sentiments, asserting that "the design, purpose and effect of the bill . . . are . . . to nullify the Fugitive Slave Law of Congress" and stating, "we cannot believe that the legislature will pass it, unless it is ready to join South Carolina and leave the Union." The *Boston Transcript* was even more alarmed, warning that "passage of [the bill] would lead to civil war, as it would bring the upholders of the United States authorities and the Union into direct collision with the state functionaries." Southerners also took note; for example, asserting that the Personal Liberty Law of 1843 had "set the example of trampling upon the laws of the land," the *Mississippian and State Gazette* observed that "[Massachusetts] now indicates her intention to pass [other statutes] of a still more odious and infamous character."

But before any action could be taken on the committee proposals, the case of Thomas Sims took center stage in the struggle over fugitive slaves in Massachusetts. Sims had been enslaved in Savannah, Georgia, until he stowed away on the brig *M. & J. C. Gilmore*, which arrived in Boston on March 6, 1851. Hoping to bring his free wife and children to Boston, Sims wired home for money and included his return address, only to have the information fall into the hands of James Potter, his erstwhile master. Potter prepared the necessary documents and then dispatched John B. Bacon to act as his agent to reclaim Sims.

Bacon arrived in Boston on Thursday, April 3, and retained the services of Seth Thomas. The same day, Thomas secured a warrant for Sims's arrest from Commissioner George Ticknor Curtis. At nine that evening, Sims was seized after a struggle with Deputy U.S. Marshal Asa O. Butman, during which Butman was stabbed in the thigh. Sims was then taken to the courthouse and detained in the custody of Marshal Charles Devens, pending a hearing on Potter's claim.

The local authorities had learned important lessons from the Minkins rescue and were determined to prevent a repeat performance. On the morning of April 4, Bostonians awoke to find that, at the direction of City Marshal Francis Tukey, the courthouse had essentially been transformed into a fortress. The building, including the main entrance, was encircled in iron chains, and the grounds were patrolled by a number of police officers (estimated variously at between 100 and 500) to ensure that only authorized people were allowed within ten feet of the building. Even Chief Justice Lemuel Shaw was forced to stoop under the chains to enter.

As news of the arrest spread and the spectacle brought a crowd of several hundred people to the courthouse square, the Vigilance Committee began its efforts to prevent the rendition of Sims. Sims's legal defense team was led by U.S. Representative Robert Rantoul Jr., an antislavery Democrat who, ironically, had been chosen to temporarily fill Daniel Webster's seat in the U.S. Senate after Webster resigned to assume the post of secretary of state. Rantoul was joined by Dana and two other experienced antislavery attorneys, Samuel E. Sewall and Charles G. Loring.

The hearing was first convened by Curtis on the morning of April 4. After Bacon and another witness identified Sims as a person enslaved to James Potter, Sewall moved to postpone the hearing for three days to allow the adequate preparation of a defense. Curtis, however, directed that the hearing would resume the following day.

In the interim, the Vigilance Committee and its allies sought to impede the rendition of Sims by other means. Sewall opened another front in the legal battle by requesting that Shaw issue a writ of habeas corpus. After a brief consultation with his colleagues of the Supreme Judicial Court, Shaw rebuffed the request, refusing to hear arguments on the constitutionality of the Fugitive Slave Act and stating that even if Sims were brought before the court, he would simply be remanded to federal custody. An effort to have the state legislature overturn this decision and order the issuance of the writ also proved unavailing.

The antislavery forces also sought to bring public pressure to bear. After being denied the use of both the Statehouse and Faneuil Hall, they organized a meeting attended by 1,000 people who initially gathered on the Boston Common, where abolitionist leader Wendell Phillips excoriated Shaw for his refusal to issue the writ of habeas corpus and advocated resistance to the Fugitive Slave Act by force if necessary. At the same time, the mayor of Boston mobilized three local military companies to deal with any potential trouble, and members of the U.S. Army posted at Charleston Navy Yard were placed on alert.

The following morning, with the courthouse still under armed guard and surrounded by crowds, Curtis heard testimony from a number of sailors from the *M. & J. C. Gilmore*, after which the claimant rested. Sims's attorneys then sought to introduce an affidavit from Sims himself, but this request was denied because the Fugitive Slave Act barred consideration of the testimony of the person being claimed. Announcing his intention to challenge the constitutionality of the Fugitive Slave Act, Rantoul then sought a postponement until the following Thursday to prepare his argument, but Curtis granted him only an additional forty-eight hours.

In the interim, a number of prominent Bostonians spoke privately to Shaw and persuaded him to hear formal arguments on the petition for habeas corpus on the morning of Monday, April 7. Although Sewall and Dana also appeared on behalf of Sims, Rantoul gave the main argument in support of the petition. Rantoul's argument relied primarily on two points. First, he asserted that the commissioners in rendition proceedings were exercising judicial authority and that this arrangement was unconstitutional because the commissioners were not appointed or compensated in the manner prescribed by article III of the Constitution. Second, Rantoul contended that, in any event, Congress did not have authority to pass legislation implementing the Fugitive Slave Clause.

In a long opinion issued the same afternoon, Shaw rejected both of these arguments. Shaw dealt first with the argument that the Constitution did not vest Congress with the authority to adopt enforcement legislation. He began his analysis by echoing Story's conception of the centrality of the Fugitive Slave Clause to the structure of the Union, observing that in a nation divided between free states and slave states, "there would of course be a constant effort of slaves to escape into free state[s]" and that, in the absence of some explicit agreement, efforts by masters to recover runaways would lead to constant tensions between the free and slave states. Focusing on the Necessary and Proper Clause and the Supremacy Clause, Shaw also emphasized the scope of federal power generally, declaring that "the general government is [armed with the power] not only to make laws regulating the rights, duties and subjects . . . confided to [it] but to administer right and justice respecting them . . . and cause them to be carried into full execution, by its own powers, without dependence upon state authority, and without any let [sic] or restraint imposed by it." Beginning with this premise, Shaw concluded that Congress possessed ample authority to adopt legislation enforcing the Fugitive Slave Clause — a conclusion, he argued, that was fortified by the near-contemporaneous action of the Congress that had passed the Fugitive Slave Act of 1793.

Turning to the claim that the 1850 statute unconstitutionally delegated federal judicial power to commissioners, Shaw conceded that, in the absence of precedent, this contention "would be entitled to very grave consideration." However, observing that the 1793 statute would be subject to the same objection, he concluded that the argument was foreclosed by *Prigg*, *Griffith*, and a variety of other precedents. Thus, Shaw held that the petition for a writ of habeas corpus must be rejected.

Despite this setback, the Vigilance Committee and its allies continued to work furiously to prevent Sims's rendition. On the same day that the Supreme Judicial Court heard arguments on the petition for habeas corpus, the rendition proceeding itself was reconvened, and Rantoul argued for six hours on Sims's behalf, reiterating the view that the Fugitive Slave Act was unconstitutional for a variety of reasons. Sewall and Loring took up the cause on Tuesday, with Sewall asserting that a telegraphic dispatch had been received stating that Sims was in fact a freeman and unsuccessfully urging Commissioner Curtis to grant a postponement to investigate this claim. Thomas then closed the case for the claimant, asserting that the Fugitive Slave Act was constitutional and noting that all the statutory prerequisites had been satisfied.

The antislavery forces also pursued a number of other options. On April 7 they procured a writ of personal replevin, commanding Devens to produce Sims for a jury trial on the claims against him. However, when served with the writ, Devens refused to surrender Sims and declared his intention to use force if necessary to prevent the putative slave from being removed from his custody. More creatively, the members of the Vigilance Committee induced Richard Hildreth, an antislavery justice of the peace, to issue an arrest warrant charging Sims with assault with intent to murder for stabbing Butman in the struggle that ensued during Sims's arrest. They reasoned that since the rendition proceeding was a civil matter, the criminal arrest warrant would take precedence, and those holding Sims would be obligated to produce him for trial in state court. Devens once again refused to produce Sims, asserting that the escaped slave was being held in federal custody not only under the authority of the Fugitive Slave Act but also under a federal criminal warrant issued by Benjamin Hallett in his capacity as a commissioner of the circuit court, alleging that Sims had committed a federal crime by assaulting Butman during the latter's efforts to enforce the statute. Devens asserted that the state warrant did not have priority over the federal warrant.

Frustrated by his inability to enforce either the writ of personal replevin or the arrest warrant, Sheriff Joseph Eveleth, with the support of Democratic governor George Boutwell, requested legal advice from state officials regarding his options. In particular, Eveleth wanted to know if he could lawfully use force to wrest Sims from federal custody. With conservative Whig attorney general John H. Clifford temporarily unavailable, the first opinion came from Samuel D. Parker, the commonwealth's attorney for Suffolk County. Parker stated definitively on April 8 that force should not be used to enforce the writ of personal replevin and that, in any event, the writ could not be used in a case in which an alleged fugitive was being held under the provisions of the Fugitive Slave Act. Parker also concluded that because Sims was being held by Devens under a federal criminal warrant as well as the Fugitive Slave Act, force could not be employed to serve the state's criminal warrant. Parker declared that "[Devens] has as much right under the laws of the land to arrest Symmes [*sic*] on a criminal warrant . . . as you have, and if he gets possession of his body first, he has the advantage of priority."

Following up on April 9, Clifford agreed with Parker on the specific issues presented by the Sims case. He also dealt at some length with the propriety of using force in a situation in which the Fugitive Slave Act was the only federal ground for holding a person who was also the subject of a state criminal warrant. In that context, Clifford vindicated the sheriff's right to use force if the federal authorities resisted the service of the state criminal process. At the same time, Clifford suggested that the sheriff make an effort to avoid armed conflict by attempting to resolve the matter through the judicial process.

With the possibility of an officially sanctioned assault foreclosed, the antislavery forces redoubled their legal efforts on behalf of Sims. After demanding a copy of the federal warrant and receiving it on Wednesday, April 10, Sewall and Charles Sumner applied to Judge Sprague for a writ of habeas corpus, alleging that the warrant was defective. Sprague—who, like Curtis and Shaw, was aligned with the so-called Hunker Whig forces—declined to issue the writ, observing that even if the criminal warrant were insufficient, Sims was being lawfully detained under the authority of the Fugitive Slave Act.

Sewall and Sumner then addressed another habeas corpus petition to Justice Levi Woodbury, sitting on circuit. Acting on behalf of Devens, conservative Whig luminaries Benjamin Robbins Curtis and Rufus Choate appeared to oppose the application. Nonetheless, on the evening of Thursday, April 10, Woodbury scheduled a hearing on the petition for the next day.

In addition to their frantic legal maneuvering, the antislavery forces continued their efforts to arouse public opinion against the Sims rendition proceedings. For example, on Friday, April 4, after being denied permission to use Faneuil Hall, the antislavery forces held a public meeting that assembled on the Boston Common and subsequently adjourned to Tremont Temple. At the meeting, approximately 1,000 Bostonians were addressed by a number of prominent antislavery activists, including Wendell Phillips, who proclaimed that the purpose of the meeting was "to arouse Massachusetts to the disgrace about to be inflicted on her, to the outrage about to be perpetrated against her laws, [and the fact that] in this effort, the State and the city officials have betrayed us and joined the enemy." A small group of protesters actively sought to organize a rescue attempt, but their plans never came to fruition.

Despite the strenuous efforts on his behalf, Thomas Sims was soon returned to slavery. On the morning of April 11, relying heavily on *Prigg*, Commissioner Curtis rejected the constitutional challenges to the Fugitive Slave Act and issued a certificate of removal that ordered Sims to be returned to the agents of James Potter. The same afternoon, after a hearing on the habeas corpus petition, Justice Woodbury remanded Sims to the custody of the federal marshal. The hearing featured a memorable exchange that began when Seth Thomas asserted that since Curtis had issued the certificate of removal, Sims was now deemed to be the ward of his master and that, as Potter's attorney, Thomas alone had the right to appear as Sims's attorney as well. Sewall responded, "that might be the law in slave states, but not in Massachusetts." Woodbury—a Democrat known for his pro-Southern perspective—asked, "[is not] Massachusetts . . . a state of the Union which recognized the institutions of slavery?" And he proclaimed to loud applause that, "for his part, he thanked God that Massachusetts was still a State of the Union."

On Saturday, April 12, Sims was transferred from the courthouse to the brig *Acorn*, which was to transport him to Savannah. Once again, the city authorities took precautions against the potential for violent outbursts against his rendition. A large force of armed police officers was brought to the courthouse, where they formed a hollow square. Sims was marched into the center of the square and escorted to the *Acorn*. Although the procession was met with jeers and catcalls, the transfer was accomplished without violence.

In general, the mainstream Boston press applauded this resolution. For example, the *Mercantile Journal* declared, "our city has shown its devotion to the Union by complying with the Constitutional compact, the maintenance of which is essential to its preservation." The *Boston Times* asserted, "this was a proceeding that will go far to wipe out the disgrace which previously came upon Boston in the case of [Shadrach Minkins]." Other newspapers focused on the blow that had been dealt to Boston abolitionists, with the *Boston Courier* proclaiming that "the reckless and unprincipled disorganizers who have been so long laboring to disturb the public peace have received the most mortifying and confounding rebuke," and the *Daily Advertiser* expressing the view that "it is a matter for congratulation that this troublesome affair . . . has terminated in a way not likely to encourage the infatuated men, who are parties to a conspiracy to defeat the execution of this [fugitive slave] law, to a repetition of similar efforts."

A variety of newspapers outside of Boston expressed similar sentiments. Not surprisingly, some of the strongest positive commentary came from the slave states. Thus, the *Fayetteville (N.C.) Observer* hailed "the triumph of law"; the *Baltimore Sun* declared, "we rejoice that Boston has . . . cleared her skirts of the infamous schemes and tricks of the fanatics and hypocritical villains, by seeing that the Constitution has been carried out and the laws vindicated"; and the *Mobile*

Daily Register asserted that "the good people of Boston . . . have . . . saved their city from a foul disgrace, and the Union from a perilous blow [and] deserve and will receive the thanks of the whole country."

Many Northern commentators outside Massachusetts were equally enthusiastic. Thus, the *Philadelphia Bulletin* proclaimed that "the tidings that the law has triumphed in Boston will be carried on the wings of the lightning, giving new confidence to patriots, North and South, in the strength and permanency of our confederacy." The *New York Journal* averred that the resolution of the Sims case has "restored our confidence in the law-abiding character of the people, and made us . . . proud of [Massachusetts]," and the *Albany Register* observed, "while we pity the hard lot which consigns [Sims] to bondage, we rejoice in the vindication of the majesty of the laws."

However, some radical voices in both the South and the North viewed the Sims affair quite differently. For example, noting the great difficulty that attended the ultimate rendition of the fugitive slave, the *Augusta Republic* asserted that "the whole case looks more like a successful farce than anything else." Similarly, while praising the efforts of those who "have nobly sustained the Constitution and the laws," the *Savannah News* observed, "if our rights, which the [Fugitive Slave Act] is designed to protect, are only to be obtained by means of the expenditure of large sums of money, by strategy and force — then the law is not worth the parchment on which it is printed."

Conversely, a significant body of Northern opinion remained unreconciled to the continued enforcement of the Fugitive Slave Act under any circumstances. The reaction of the radical antislavery press reflected this viewpoint. Thus, the *Liberator* declared that "such a week Boston has never passed through in her history — certainly not since the revolutionary struggle — so humiliating, so disgraceful, so appalling," and the *Christian Secretary* of Hartford, Connecticut, lamented that "Boston men once loved liberty, and would pour out their blood like water in defense of it. . . . But things have changed now." Similarly, the *National Era* described the Sims affair as "a disgusting business" and asserted that "the less said about it, the better for the honor of the country."

Perhaps most significantly, a state legislative committee once again aligned itself firmly with the radical antislavery forces. On April 9 — two days before Curtis issued his decision in the case — a committee had been impaneled by the senate to investigate the events surrounding the conflict over the rendition. The committee, chaired by antislavery Democrat Frederick Robinson, then held extensive hearings in which many of the key players in the controversy were questioned in detail about their actions. However, the most dramatic confrontation came during the testimony of Benjamin Hallett, who was questioned about the federal warrant he had issued charging Sims with criminal assault on Asa Butman.

Hallett's defiant testimony gave no details about the disposition of those federal criminal charges, but he declared that his actions and those of other federal officials "will meet with the approbation of all, from the President, through Congress, down to the Supreme Court and the minds of the majority." At the same time, Hallett took the opportunity to deride the proceedings of the committee itself, asserting that its mission was "to get up a conflict between the legislative and judicial functions." He also made no secret of his contempt for the antislavery forces, sneering, "I have no sympathy with the pretended philanthropy, which would depend on sham warrants to remove a criminal from the hands of a national officer . . . and it is really wonderful why philanthropy wished to send [Sims] to State's Prison." At the conclusion of Hallett's testimony, Robinson observed, "if the State pays you for giving evidence, it will do so for nothing," and Hallett replied, "if I have been so fortunate . . . as to teach the chairman of the Committee to pay a due regard to the law of the land . . . my labor will not have been in vain."

Not surprisingly, the tone of the committee report issued by Robinson on April 22 was quite different. The report began by excoriating the Boston authorities for effectuating the initial arrest of Sims. Noting that the Personal Liberty Law of 1843 explicitly prohibited city and state officials from aiding in the enforcement of the Fugitive Slave Act of 1793, the committee asserted that city officials' decision to make the arrest "amount[ed] to an armed resistance to the execution of the laws of the State." Though conceding that the police might have acted under the "pretence" that Sims had stolen a watch, the committee brushed aside the relevance of this possibility because it did not appear "directly" in the testimony taken. The report also discounted Tukey's claim that the participation of city police officers had been necessary to forestall "riot and bloodshed" that might have ensued if Potter's agents had attempted to detain Sims, contending that "it did not appear that any arrest could have been made, or that any riot or bloodshed could have followed, if the city authorities had not interfered."

The report criticized Devens's refusal to produce Sims in response to the writ of personal replevin. Notwithstanding the fact that Shaw had held in the *Latimer* case that such a writ could not be enforced when a putative slave was being held under the terms of the Fugitive Slave Act, the committee contended that Devens should have produced Sims for a jury trial and then challenged the use of the writ in state court, appealing if necessary to the Supreme Court if the state court ruled against him. At the very least, this approach would have substantially delayed the rendition process. Nonetheless, the committee insisted that the claimant's rights would have been fully protected by the bond required to be posted as a prerequisite for obtaining the writ.

The report's harshest language, however, was reserved for the use of the federal criminal warrant to block Sims's release into state custody. In addition to excoriating Hallett for his "utter contempt for the Legislature, Constitution and the laws of the state," the committee's portrayal of the conflict between the federal and state warrants was the mirror image of that which Hallett had presented. The report observed that "the criminal process of the State was in due form under oath, and was issued against a person who confessed that he had committed a high crime against laws of the State," and "the efforts made to serve it prove that it was issued in good faith." By contrast, the report contended that the federal warrant was used "as a cover to enable the claimant of a fugitive slave to carry him out of [Massachusetts] while charged with crime against the laws thereof" and, as such, constituted "a gross contempt of state sovereignty." Indeed, the report asserted that to vindicate "the great doctrine of State rights," city officials should have raised an armed force to serve the state criminal warrant on Sims after he had been taken to the *Acorn*, and Hallett would have borne the responsibility for any bloodshed that ensued. Echoing the previous proposals in the Buckingham report, the committee called for new legislation that would prevent Massachusetts officials from participating in the rendition of fugitive slaves in the future.

However, the state senate as a whole proved unwilling to adopt such measures. On May 21, constitutional concerns led the senate to strip away the habeas corpus and jury trial provisions by a vote of 17–16. The amended bill was then defeated 16–13. Both houses did, however, overwhelmingly adopt a resolution condemning the Fugitive Slave Act as "hostile to the sentiments of Christianity and abhorrent to the feelings of the people of [Massachusetts]" and declaring that "such a law will naturally fail to secure that support in the heart and conscience of the community without which any law must, sooner or later, become a dead letter." But at the same time, the resolution reaffirmed the legislature's opposition to the doctrine of nullification. The following year, another effort was made to pass a sweeping personal liberty law, but the bill was narrowly rejected by the state house of representatives. Similarly, the state constitutional convention convened in 1853 refused to adopt a proposal by Richard Henry Dana that would have required state courts to grant petitions for writs of habeas corpus in fugitive slave cases.

In the interim, urged on by Daniel Webster, U.S. District Attorney George Lunt continued to prosecute several people who had allegedly participated in the rescue of Shadrach Minkins. Justice Benjamin Robbins Curtis and Judge Peleg Sprague presided over the trials. Not surprisingly, given their political orientation, neither was sympathetic to the constitutional claims of the antislavery forces, although there is no indication that they treated the defendants unfairly. For example, in his charge to the jury in the trial of James Scott, Sprague firmly rejected the contention that he should hold the Fugitive Slave Act of 1850 unconstitutional. Apparently viewing the 1850 statute as indistinguishable from the 1793 act for constitutional purposes, Sprague first reviewed both the background of the 1793 statute and the extensive case law that had rejected constitutional challenges to it. He then asserted:

> To overturn the construction of the Constitution so established, would be a most dangerous violation of principle and duty. If a court may do this, it may overturn established rules of property, of personal rights, and of evidence upon which the community have for a long time acted, and thus shake every man's title, put in jeopardy every man's liberty, and render the law so uncertain that no counsel could advise, and no man act with safety.

Similarly, at the trial of Thomas Morris in November 1851, Curtis firmly rejected the argument that juries should be free to disregard judges' rulings on issues of law and come to an independent decision on the statutory and constitutional issues raised by the case—in effect, to engage in jury nullification—instead charging the jury that it was bound by the rules of law established by judges.

But despite such rulings, none of those charged in the Minkins rescue were convicted. Some of the acquittals simply reflected the weakness of the government's case against the specific defendants. Moreover, all the defendants were ably represented by antislavery attorneys such as Richard Henry Dana and John P. Hale. But other factors were at work as well.

The evidence against James Scott, who was tried in May 1851, and Lewis Hayden, whose trial took place the following month, was particularly strong. In each case, a number of prosecution witnesses positively identified the defendant as a participant or leader in the rescue effort. Moreover, Thomas Murray, the taxicab driver who transported Hayden and Minkins to Cambridge, testified that Hayden had offered him a bribe to make himself unavailable to appear at the trial. However, Dana and Hale produced witnesses who claimed to have seen the defendants elsewhere at the time of the rescue. Against this background, even though an author sympathetic to the rescuers characterized the defense evidence in the Scott case as "unpersuasive," two jurors adamantly held out for acquittal, creating a hung jury. The Hayden case ended in a similar deadlock, with three jurors refusing to vote to convict.

The outcomes of the Scott and Hayden trials were an apt reflection of public opinion in Boston in 1852. Many Bostonians were willing to acquiesce in the enforcement of the Fugitive Slave Act (albeit reluctantly in many cases). But while the political and economic elite of the city as a whole appears to have been less committed to antislavery principles than the citizenry in other parts of Massachusetts, a substantial minority of Boston residents was determined to aggressively resist the rendition of fugitive slaves. Indeed, the Minkins case demonstrated that some were willing to resort to violence to prevent rendition.

Against the background of the tumult surrounding the Craft, Minkins, and Sims cases, it would have been a brave slaveholder indeed who ventured to Boston to recover an escaped slave in the early 1850s. In any event, more than three years passed between the rendition of Thomas Sims and the next confrontation in Boston over an individual fugitive. Nonetheless, in the interim, the fugitive slave controversy continued to roil the political landscape at both the national and state levels.

Indeed, the presidential campaign of 1852 revolved largely around the question of whether the Compromise of 1850 in general and the Fugitive Slave Act in particular should be viewed as a final, permanent settlement of the sectional conflict. While both the Democratic nominee Franklin Pierce and the Democratic platform unequivocally endorsed the concept of finality, the situation of the Whigs was more complex. The pro-compromise forces controlled a majority of the delegates to the Whig convention and succeeded in having the principle of finality ensconced in the party platform. But supporters of the compromise were split between Fillmore and Webster, and Winfield Scott was ultimately chosen as the party's nominee. When Scott refused to unequivocally endorse the compromise, the election became in substantial measure a referendum on finality.

Nationally, the election was a disaster for the Whigs, as Pierce won an overwhelming victory. At the same time, the returns provided another illustration of the strength of antislavery sentiment in Massachusetts, where Scott handily defeated Pierce. In addition, Free-Soil candidate John P. Hale received 22 percent of the vote in Massachusetts – the largest Free-Soil vote in any state – on a platform that explicitly demanded repeal of the Fugitive Slave Act. The pro-compromise forces suffered another blow with the death of their leader, Daniel Webster, on October 24.

Hale's performance in Massachusetts was impressive, but voters' overwhelming preference for candidates of the mainstream parties reflected the limited influence of those who advocated aggressive resistance to the Fugitive Slave Act in the period 1851 to 1853. Those limits were also clearly reflected in the proceedings of the state constitutional convention that was convened in Boston on May 4, 1853.

Although the dispute over slavery was not the major impetus for the convention, delegates who opposed the Fugitive Slave Act tried to use the occasion to advance their cause in two different ways. First, they sought to arm juries with the right to make independent assessments of the law, reasoning that some jurors would use this authority to conclude that the Fugitive Slave Act was unconstitutional. However, this proposal was defeated, as even some antislavery stalwarts such as Richard Henry Dana were loathe to reallocate authority from judges to juries. Second, reacting to the Sims decision, Dana moved to require that judges rule favorably on all habeas corpus petitions, except in cases in which the legislature had explicitly granted discretion to the court. The convention also rejected this proposal in the face of Hallett's assertion that it might lead to conflicts between the state and the federal government in cases involving fugitive slaves. Thus, the legal backdrop for the struggle over fugitive slaves in Massachusetts remained unchanged.

By contrast, 1854 witnessed a dramatic change in the political context of the struggle. Ironically, the catalyst for this change did not directly involve fugitive slaves at all; rather, the trigger was the introduction of the Kansas-Nebraska bill by Senator Stephen A. Douglas of Illinois in January 1854. By its terms, the bill overturned the provision of the Missouri Compromise that had barred the introduction of slavery into the northern portion of the Louisiana Purchase since 1820 and proposed to organize the Kansas and Nebraska territories under a regime of popular sovereignty. Thus, the bill reignited the explosive issue of slavery in the territories.

The introduction of the Kansas-Nebraska bill created a firestorm in the North. Many Northerners viewed the effort to repeal the Missouri Compromise as a breach of faith that undermined the premises on which the concept of finality was based. Thus, Amos Lawrence, a conservative Boston Whig who had hitherto supported the Compromise of 1850, warned that if additional territories were opened to slavery, the Fugitive Slave Act would become a "dead letter" in the free states. Nonetheless, the bill easily passed the Senate on March 4, 1854. After a bitter political struggle, the House of Representatives concurred on May 22, and Franklin Pierce signed the bill into law on May 30. Coincidentally, only six days earlier, a fugitive slave named Anthony Burns had been seized on the streets of Boston.

CHAPTER 4

Anthony Burns: Escape, Capture, and Failed Rescue

Anthony Burns was born in 1833 in Stafford Court House, a small village in Stafford County, Virginia. Burns was the youngest of thirteen children born to a slave employed as a cook by John Suttle. When Suttle died, his widow moved Burns and his family to Acquia, a small village five or six miles north of Stafford Court House. Mrs. Suttle died when Burns was six, after which he was enslaved to Charles F. Suttle, a shopkeeper and sheriff who also served in the Virginia legislature.

From the age of seven, Burns was hired out to a succession of temporary masters, each of whom paid Suttle a fee for the right to Burns's labor for a year. While working in a sawmill at the age of twelve or thirteen, Burns was seriously injured, suffering a mangled hand. While convalescing from his injuries, Burns became intensely interested in Christianity. After recovering, he was baptized and soon became a lay minister in the slave community. In contravention of Virginia law, Burns also persuaded a young woman to teach him how to read and write, and for a time he conducted classes to pass on that knowledge to other slaves.

In 1853 Burns's circumstances changed dramatically. Suttle sent Burns to Richmond, where William Brent, who had previously purchased Burns's services for two years, was given the responsibility for hiring Burns out. The following year Burns was hired out to a pharmacist named Millspaugh, but when Millspaugh unexpectedly found that he did not have enough work to keep Burns fully occupied, he and Burns entered into an illegal arrangement: Burns would seek short-term employment and pay Millspaugh a certain amount periodically, keeping any excess earnings for himself. Taking advantage of the freedom afforded to him by this arrangement, Burns enlisted the aid of a sympathetic sailor and stowed away on a ship bound for Boston in early February 1854. He arrived in Boston in late February or early March and procured employment as a cook on a mud scow, but he lost that position due to an inability to bake bread properly. Burns then worked temporarily cleaning windows at the Mattapan Iron Works before finding permanent employment in a local clothing store, where he worked until his recapture.

Burns's undoing was a letter he wrote to his brother, who remained enslaved in Richmond. Seeking to keep his whereabouts secret, Burns took the necessary steps to have the letter postmarked in Canada, but the letter's content carelessly indicated its origin in Boston. His brother's master came into possession of the letter and conveyed it to Suttle. With the evidence of Burns's location in hand, Suttle asserted his claim to recover the erstwhile slave in the state circuit court for Alexandria County, Virginia. On May 16 the court produced a transcript describing Burns and declaring that Suttle had provided "satisfactory proof" that Burns did in fact owe service to Suttle. By obtaining this order, Suttle hoped to take advantage of section 10 of the Fugitive Slave Act, which provided that in a rendition proceeding, such a transcript would be "full and conclusive evidence of the fact of escape, and that the service or labor of the person escaping is due to the party in such record mentioned." Armed with the court document, Suttle, accompanied by Brent, set off for Boston and appeared before Commissioner Edward Greely Loring on May 24, 1854.

Loring was born in Marblehead, Massachusetts, on January 28, 1802. His father died less than a year later, and his mother was soon remarried to Thomas Curtis, a Boston merchant who had been a junior business partner of the Lorings. Thus Loring became related by marriage to what was to become one of the most powerful conservative Whig families in Boston, numbering among his cousins luminaries such as Justice Benjamin Robbins Curtis and Commissioner George Ticknor Curtis.

After graduating from Harvard in 1822, Loring opened a law partnership with Horace Mann in 1832. Loring soon entered politics and became associated with a progressive faction of the nascent Whig Party known as the Young Men of Boston. Beginning in 1836 he served three one-year terms in the lower house of the Massachusetts legislature. Loring's career in the legislature ended in 1838 when Governor Edward Everett appointed him to serve as a master in the Suffolk County chancery court. During this period Loring was also a justice of the peace, and in 1841 Justice Story appointed him a commissioner of the federal court of claims. Reappointment to the Suffolk County post was normally a matter of routine, but when the Democratic governor and executive council declined to reappoint Loring in 1843, he saw himself as a political martyr.

Despite his disappointment, Loring remained actively engaged in public affairs. For the next several years he expended much of his energy in support of Horace Mann's movement to reform the system of public education in Massachusetts, representing the Seventh Ward on Boston's Public School Committee for two years. In that capacity Loring led the successful effort to change the system for selecting teachers, replacing an informal process that was widely viewed as being rife with cronyism with a formal procedure to evaluate all applicants.

However, the political relationship between Mann and Loring did not survive the escalation of the dispute over slavery in the late 1840s. While Mann became a stalwart of the Free-Soil Party in Massachusetts, Loring—like the Curtis family generally—was a staunch supporter of Daniel Webster and the Compromise of 1850. Indeed, Loring openly defended the constitutionality of the Fugitive Slave Act in a series of articles in the *Boston Daily Advertiser*. During the same period, Loring's professional life and financial situation took a sharp turn for the better. In 1847, with the strong support of the Curtises, Loring was appointed probate judge in Suffolk County. Subsequently, when an associate lecturer resigned from the Harvard Law School faculty in 1852, Loring was chosen to replace him. Although the university's Board of Overseers subsequently refused the law school's request to make Loring a full professor, he was reappointed without incident to the lecturer's position the following year. At the same time, Loring continued to function as a commissioner in federal court. It was in this capacity that he became involved in the case of Anthony Burns.

Once Suttle approached him with the record from the Virginia court, the Fugitive Slave Act left the commissioner with no discretion. Loring issued an arrest warrant authorizing U.S. Marshal Watson Freeman to arrest Burns and bring him before Loring for a hearing. Freeman entrusted execution of the warrant to Deputy Marshal Asa O. Butman—the same man who had been instrumental in arresting Thomas Sims.

That evening, soon after Burns left work, Butman grabbed him by the shoulder. Seeking to avoid the kind of public struggle that had attended the arrest of Sims, Butman told Burns that he was being arrested for robbing a jewelry store and was to be brought before his accuser. Confident of his innocence on that charge, Burns put up no resistance. Nonetheless, he was quickly surrounded by six or seven other men, who carried him bodily to the Boston courthouse. There, they were greeted by Freeman, who was standing with a drawn sword on the steps outside. Burns was then carried into the courthouse and up several flights of stairs to the jury room. After first expressing surprise that the jeweler was not present, it soon became apparent to Burns that he had in fact been seized as a fugitive slave.

Twenty minutes later, Suttle and Brent entered the room. Suttle approached Burns, doffed his hat, and said, "How do you do, Mr. Burns?" Suttle then asked Burns, "Why did you run away?"

Burns replied, "I fell asleep on board the vessel where I worked and, before I woke up, she set sail and carried me off."

Suttle asked, "Haven't I always treated you well, Tony? Haven't I always given you money when you needed?"

Burns stated, "You have always given me twelve and one-half cents once a year."

After informing Freeman that the prisoner was in fact the man they sought, Suttle and Brent left the room.

Burns and his captors spent the night of May 24 in the jury room with the door barred. The hearing on Suttle's claim was scheduled for the next morning. Suttle, Brent, and the marshals no doubt hoped that Burns could be quietly returned to slavery without creating the public uproar that had accompanied the Sims rendition and had led to the successful rescue of Shadrach Minkins.

These hopes were soon dashed, however. By 7:30 the next morning, the Reverend Leonard Grimes, minister of the Baptist church that Burns attended in Boston, had become aware of his arrest. After relaying the information to Theodore Parker, Grimes hurried to the courthouse, arriving shortly before the rendition hearing was scheduled to begin, and was given a pass to enter the jury room. Grimes was soon joined in the courtroom by a number of other members of the Vigilance Committee.

Serendipitously, Richard Henry Dana, the antislavery lawyer who had participated in the legal defense of both Minkins and Sims, was in the vicinity of the courthouse when a passerby told him an escaped slave was in custody and about to be tried. Dana quickly made his way to the jury room and offered his services to Burns. Burns initially refused the offer, stating, "it was no use," and observing, "they will swear to me and get me back, and if they do, I shall fare worse if I resist."

Dana later recalled that he considered it inappropriate to press a defense on an unwilling client, and in any event, the best course for Burns might in fact be a quiet return to Suttle. Nonetheless, Dana observed that Burns's mental and emotional state rendered him unfit to defend himself, and he spoke privately with Loring, urging him not to act hastily but to speak to Burns confidentially, out of earshot of Suttle and his representatives. After receiving appropriate assurances from Loring, Dana left and went to his office. There he was visited by Theodore Parker, who convinced Dana to at least attend the hearing. Parker and Dana then returned together to the courthouse.

By the time they arrived at about nine o'clock, the hearing was already under way. Suttle was represented by Seth J. Thomas, who had also represented the claimants in the Minkins and Sims proceedings, and by Edward Griffin Parker, who was beginning to present the basis for Suttle's claim when Dana and Theodore Parker entered the room. There they encountered abolitionist Wendell Phillips, and Dana reiterated the fact that he had not been retained as counsel and opined that his assistance was far more likely to cause Burns more pain and suffering than to prevent his rendition.

The Reverend Parker, however, refused to acquiesce quietly in Dana's decision. He approached Burns and, describing himself as a minister at large on behalf of fugitive slaves, asked the alleged fugitive if he wanted counsel. At first, Burns remained committed to his initial position. Observing that he had already been identified by Suttle as an escaped slave, Burns stated, "if I must go back, I want to go back as easy as I can." But Parker persisted, assuring Burns that it would do no harm to mount a defense, and Burns finally stated, "you may do as you have a mind about it."

Armed with this somewhat ambiguous response, Parker made another effort to persuade Dana to serve as Burns's counsel. Dana once again demurred, as did Charles M. Ellis, another Vigilance Committee attorney in attendance at the hearing. Thus it seemed that

Burns might well be returned to the service of Suttle without ever mounting a legal defense.

The situation changed dramatically after Suttle's counsel completed the submission of their documentary evidence and called William Brent as a witness. Dana sat silent while Brent described his interactions with Burns in Richmond and stated that Burns had left Richmond "on or about the 24th day of March last." But when Brent was asked to recount Burns's admissions from the night before, Dana sprang to his feet and requested permission to address the proceeding as an amicus curiae. Asserting that Burns "is not in a condition to determine whether he will have counsel or not, or whether or not and how he shall appear in his defense," Dana moved for a postponement to allow "the prisoner to recover himself from the stupefaction of his sudden arrest, and his novel and distressing situation, and to have opportunity to consult with friends and members of the bar, and to determine what course he will pursue." Attorney Parker objected to the motion, noting the inconvenience and expense that any delay would cause his clients. Dana responded by reminding Loring of the "immense stake of freedom or slavery for life at issue" and argued, "we cannot weigh liberty against convenience and freedom against pecuniary expense."

At this point, Loring called Burns forward, asked him if he wished to mount a defense, and advised him that he had a right to counsel. When Burns made no immediate reply, Loring asked Burns if he wished to come back tomorrow or the next day and make his decision at that time. When Burns responded that he would like the extra time, Loring said, "then you shall have it," essentially indicating that Dana's motion would be granted.

The only question remaining was whether the hearing would reconvene on Friday or Saturday. Marshal Freeman whispered something in Loring's ear, apparently pressing for as short a postponement as possible. Loring first responded, "No, Sir, he must have the time necessary." When Freeman persisted, Loring firmly replied, "I can't help that, Sir, he shall have the proper time," and ordered that the hearing be reconvened on the morning of Saturday, May 27.

The delay allowed Burns's supporters time to organize resistance to the rendition on a variety of fronts. Dana petitioned Judge Peleg Sprague for a writ of personal replevin, but Sprague rebuffed the petition on the ground that federal courts did not issue such writs. Seth Webb Jr., another Vigilance Committee lawyer, was more successful in state court, persuading Judge Daniel Wells of the Massachusetts Court of Common Pleas to issue the writ. However, Freeman simply ignored the order. In the name of African American abolitionist minister Lewis Hayden, Webb also filed a tort action against Suttle and Brent, charging that they had unlawfully conspired to arrest and imprison Burns and remove him to Alexandria, Virginia. Suttle and Brent were each forced to post bond of $5,000 to avoid detention.

In addition, on the morning of Friday, May 26, the Vigilance Committee met to plot a course of popular resistance to the rendition of Burns. All agreed that a large public meeting should be held at seven o'clock that evening, but the committee was split between those who urged that resistance be limited to nonviolent public protests and those who advocated a direct assault on the courthouse to free Burns. A "rescue committee" composed of about thirty supporters of a direct assault convened separately and chose a six-person executive committee to plan the details of the attack. This committee included Wendell Phillips, Theodore Parker, Thomas Whitworth Higginson, Henry Kemp, Samuel Gridley Howe, and Austin Bearse. Higginson, pastor of the Free Church of Worcester and a veteran of the unsuccessful effort to free Thomas Sims, was selected to chair the meeting.

At first, the proponents of direct action seemed predisposed to a nighttime attack on the courthouse. But as the day wore on, sentiment shifted toward the idea of an assault on Saturday morning, while the formal hearing on Burns's rendition was taking place. The theory was that a large crowd of antislavery advocates would be gathering outside the courthouse at that time in any event, and many of those present would join the rescue effort. Still, no detailed plan had been formulated when Higginson left to meet Martin Stowell, a fellow abolitionist who was arriving by train from Worcester at six o'clock, one hour before the public protest was to take place at Faneuil Hall.

When Higginson told him of the rescue plan, Stowell immediately expressed great reservations. Stowell argued that the rescue effort would not succeed unless it was given momentum by other forces. After some discussion, he and Higginson agreed that the best plan would be to have a body of rescuers waiting near the courthouse when the mass protest meeting was taking place, send an emissary to the meeting to announce that a "mob of negroes" was already attacking the courthouse, and then have Phillips or some other speaker urge the crowd to join the attack. Although Higginson never had the opportunity to present this plan to the rescue committee as a group, he received quick approval from Parker and Howe and reluctant acquiescence from Kemp.

Higginson and Stowell then began making preparations for the attack. Higginson purchased half a dozen axes, while Stowell recruited ten men to provide the nucleus of attackers, to which Lewis Hayden added ten more and Kemp added five. John L. Swift, "a young man full of zeal with a stentorian voice," was chosen to proclaim to the mass meeting that an attack was under way.

While Higginson, Stowell, and their associates were planning the rescue efforts, the remainder of the Vigilance Committee and its allies were busily publicizing the rendition proceedings and the mass protest meeting. For example, one printed appeal decried the spectacle "of a man . . . chained like a felon in a Boston court house . . . awaiting the mockery of a trial which shall doom him to all the unutterable misery, horror, and blackness of darkness faintly shadowed beneath that word — SLAVERY! — without once allowing him to see the face of a judge [or] the face of a jury" and implored the people to "leave your fields, your work-shops, your stores, your home, leave every occupation, duty, and pleasure and swarm to Boston!" Responding to these appeals, a crowd variously estimated at between 2,000 and 5,000 people gathered in Faneuil Hall at seven o'clock to protest the rendition proceedings.

The crowd was treated to a series of speeches by Wendell Phillips, Theodore Parker, and others that denounced both the rendition of Burns specifically and the Fugitive Slave Act generally in the most inflammatory language imaginable. Phillips, for example, praised the people of Pennsylvania for killing a slave owner who had sought to recover a fugitive from service and asserted that "if [Anthony Burns] leaves the city of Boston, Massachusetts is a conquered State." Sounding the same theme, Parker began his speech by addressing the crowd as "fellow subjects of Virginia" and declaring, "I will take it back when you show me the fact is not so." Parker then proclaimed that what was needed was "to have deeds, as well as words."

Parker ended his speech by calling for the crowd to reassemble at the courthouse at nine o'clock on Saturday morning. By this time, many at the Faneuil Hall gathering were calling loudly for an immediate assault to free Burns. But Phillips supported Parker's plan. While declaring, "whenever there is a fair probability of saving a slave from the hands of those who call themselves the officers of the law, by trampling under foot any statute, or any man, I will be ready to help any hundred men to do it," he pleaded for the crowd "not [to be] carried away by a momentary impulse, to a fatal indiscretion, which shall wreck the ship which may yet be piloted into a safe and successful harbor." Instead, he counseled, "let us go home to-night, fellow citizens. The zeal that will not keep till to-morrow, never will free a slave."

Initially, it appeared that Phillips had been successful in averting an immediate assault on the court. But at this point, an unidentified man (probably Swift) loudly proclaimed that "a large body of negroes were assembled in Court Square, determined to rescue the fugitive to-night." This announcement had precisely the effect that Stowell and Higginson had expected. Without any formal leaders, a large portion of the Faneuil Hall crowd immediately left the meeting, and by shortly after 9:30, several hundred protesters had gathered outside the courthouse. However, none of the leaders of the Faneuil Hall meeting were among them.

Kemp advised Higginson to wait for more reinforcements before attempting to rescue Burns. But with no one clearly in charge, Stowell began to distribute the axes. In addition, Stowell, Higginson, Hayden, Webb, and a number of other men began to use a wooden beam taken from a local construction site as a battering ram, attempting to breach the double doors on the west side of the courthouse that opened on the steps leading up to the jury room where Burns was being held.

At the time the assault began, Burns was being guarded by forty to fifty temporary deputies who had been hired by Freeman to thwart any rescue attempt. Freemen took a group of fifteen deputies to the entryway that was under assault. At the same time, heads were seen at open windows on the third floor of the courthouse. A number of shots were fired. Although many observers reported that most of the shots had come from Burns's guards, the majority of the damage was done to the courthouse itself.

In any event, the protesters with the battering ram ultimately succeeded in breaching the doorway. A brief scuffle between the protesters and the guards ensued, during which James Batchelder, one of the temporary deputies, was killed. Batchelder, a twenty-four-year-old customhouse truckman, had been bracing the door when the battering ram broke through. During the ensuing combat, Batchelder exclaimed, "I am stabbed," and staggered backward with a wound in the groin. Notwithstanding this exclamation, another guard believed that Batchelder had been shot. Whatever the cause of the wound, Batchelder died moments later.

Despite their successful breach of the doorway, the wielders of the battering ram were beaten back, with Stowell and Hayden firing shots to cover the retreat of their compatriots. After this setback, the protest at the courthouse quickly lost its momentum. Bloody from his struggle with the guards, Higginson exclaimed to the crowd, "You cowards, will you desert us now?" The police soon arrived and arrested a handful of demonstrators, including Stowell, who was apprehended trying to break through the door again, this time with an ax. Thus, the effort to forcibly rescue Anthony Burns ended in failure.

In the wake of the events of Friday night, the government authorities quickly took steps to ensure that any further rescue attempts would be equally unavailing. At the Faneuil Hall meeting, Wendell Phillips had praised Boston mayor Jerome Van Crowninshield Smith for refusing to cooperate with the rendition proceedings. Now, however, Smith called out the state militia to guard the courthouse, and by shortly after midnight, the area had been cleared of civilians. In addition, Freeman enlisted the aid of a contingent of marines quartered at the Charlestown Navy Yard and also dispatched the steamer *John Taylor* to bring additional marines from nearby Fort Independence. Freeman then sent a telegram to President Franklin Pierce, informing him of the attack, detailing Freeman's subsequent actions, and declaring, "Every thing is now quiet. The attack was repulsed by my own guard." Pierce responded: "Your conduct is approved. The law must be executed."

The events of the night of May 26 were widely reported, and reactions were divided along predictable lines. Conservatives were outraged by the assault on the courthouse. For example, the *Boston Journal* declared:

> if unrestrained passion is to be allowed full sway — if lawless violence is to go unrebuked, and men in high social position are to

become the leaders of a mob – if a law of the United States is to be trampled under foot, and the officers of the government shot down in the discharge of their duty, and this without rebuke, then indeed will a blot rest upon the fair fame of our city, and Boston will be degraded in the estimation of the whole Union.

By contrast, the abolitionist *National Era* linked the resistance to the passions inflamed by the Kansas-Nebraska Act and asserted that the rescue effort "ha[d] its roots in the noblest feelings of the human heart – in a regard for the rights of man, in a love of liberty, in a high appreciation of the ordinary safeguards and guaranties of liberty."

The members of the Vigilance Committee clearly shared the latter sentiments. Nonetheless, faced with the heavy military presence, the committee concluded early on the morning of Saturday, May 27, that no further efforts should be made to assault the courthouse. In addition, Mayor Smith had posters distributed urging the citizenry to cooperate with the authorities in the maintenance of peace and good order. Nonetheless, on Saturday morning, a crowd estimated at several thousand gathered near the courthouse.

It was against this background that the hearing before Loring resumed at ten o'clock. In the interim, armed with a promise from conservative Whig industrialist Amos Lawrence to defray the costs of additional representation, Dana had attempted to persuade other prominent Boston attorneys to serve as his co-counsel. However, Judge Richard Fletcher was otherwise occupied, and abolitionist attorney Charles G. Loring (a cousin of the commissioner) was out of town. After conservative Whig Rufus Choate also refused to join the defense team, Dana settled on Charles Mayo Ellis, a young attorney who volunteered his services.

After Loring convened the hearing on Saturday, Ellis immediately moved for an additional delay, noting that Dana had obtained access to Burns only the previous day and that Ellis himself had never even had an opportunity to speak to Burns. Asserting that Burns "stands here as a freeman" and that "this was the only tribunal standing between the man and perpetual slavery," Ellis contended that Burns's attorneys needed more time to prepare their defense. While expressing his disapproval of the attack on the courthouse, Ellis also cited the "excitement" of the morning as a reason for granting his motion.

Parker and Thomas objected to any further postponements. Asserting that there was no reason for delay, Parker observed that the proceeding was only in the nature of a preliminary hearing, not a final determination of Burns's status. Thomas emphasized what he saw as the strength of the claimant's case, declaring that "[Burns] had no defense to make to the claim." Thomas also asserted that a continuance would only increase the likelihood of further "excitement" and took the opportunity to declare that violent opposition to the operation of the Fugitive Slave Act was treasonous.

Dana responded to these arguments by observing that he was asking for a much shorter delay than had been granted in the Sims case. He also reiterated that it had been less than twenty-four hours since Burns had agreed to be represented by counsel. Finally, like Ellis before him, Dana emphasized the serious consequences of a decision against the defendant, noting that if Suttle prevailed, he did not have to return Burns to Virginia but could take him to "Texas, the coast of Africa, or [a slave market in] New Orleans." Obviously impressed with these arguments, and averring that Burns "is as yet to be regarded as a freeman," Loring granted the defense motion and delayed the start of the hearing until Monday, May 29.

On a different legal front, Stowell and seven others were arraigned in police court for allegedly shooting and killing Batchelder. Luther A. Ham, the deputy police chief who filed the complaint, moved for a postponement of the hearing on the charges until Wednesday, May 31. Representing the defendants, attorney Charles G. Evans objected that some of his clients were being indiscriminately charged with murder to ensure that they would be denied bail. Nonetheless, the judge postponed the hearing until Tuesday and ordered all the defendants held in jail until the proceedings reconvened.

At the same time, Leonard Grimes was making feverish efforts to raise funds to purchase Burns's freedom from Suttle. At the morning hearing, responding to Dana's assertion that Suttle might sell Burns at a slave market, Edward Parker had declared that Suttle was willing to sell Burns in Boston. Initially, both Parker and Suttle took the position that the sale could take place only after Suttle's claim under the Fugitive Slave Act had been vindicated. After meeting with Grimes, however, Suttle agreed that the sale could take place before the formal adjudication of his claim and agreed on a price of $1,200. Parker informed Grimes that the offer to sell Burns was binding only if the transaction could be consummated on Saturday, leaving Grimes less than a day to raise the necessary funds.

Working under this intense time pressure, Grimes faced some initial setbacks in his efforts to obtain the necessary funds. He first approached a former supporter of the Fugitive Slave Act (whose name has not survived) who had been overheard saying that he would contribute $100 toward the purchase of Burns's freedom. Though admitting that he had made such a pledge, the potential donor stated that he had been dissuaded from making any contribution by Benjamin Hallett, who adamantly opposed any sale of Burns prior to a decision in the rendition proceedings. However, the same person offered to contribute after Burns was returned to Virginia. Grimes was equally unsuccessful in his solicitation of Abbott Lawrence, a prominent Boston philanthropist who denounced the Fugitive Slave Act as an "infamous" statute but declined to contribute because he felt that doing so would implicitly endorse the statute.

Despite continued efforts by Hallett to discourage contributions, Grimes's efforts met greater success as the day wore on. Although a number of abolitionists such as Theodore Parker and William Lloyd Garrison objected in principle to paying slave owners to obtain the freedom of men such as Burns, Grimes was able to secure pledges from a variety of other wealthy Bostonians. Conservative Whigs were among the most prominent contributors. Thomas B. and Charles P. Curtis — the stepbrothers of Edward Loring — were particularly generous in their support of the effort, and Samuel A. Eliot, the only Massachusetts congressman to vote in favor of the Fugitive Slave Act, also contributed. Based on these and other pledges, by 11 PM, Grimes had obtained a check for $400 from Edward Parker himself and a check for $800 from Hamilton Willis, a wealthy retired businessman. Grimes next took the checks to Revere House, where Suttle gave final approval to the sale and authorized his lawyers to sign the relevant documents on his behalf. Grimes, Parker, and Thomas then brought the checks to Loring's office, where Loring drafted a deed of manumission for Burns. Burns's supporters were so confident at this point that a carriage was waiting to bring him to Grimes's residence.

Loring then sent a message summoning Marshal Freeman to his office, but Freeman replied that he could not come. At Loring's suggestion, he, Grimes, Parker, and Thomas went to Freeman's office, where they found both Freeman and Hallett. Hallett raised a number of objections to the proposed sale. First, he complained that if the sale were consummated at that point, the law would be evaded, and neither the federal government nor the state would be responsible for the expenses that had already been incurred. Loring responded by reading a section of the Fugitive Slave Act that refuted this claim. Hallett then argued that the transaction would be illegal under the Massachusetts law that prohibited the sale of slaves. Loring brushed aside this complaint as well, noting that the law was aimed not against selling a man into freedom but against selling him into slavery, and Grimes exclaimed, "I will take the penalty."

Although Hallett's substantive objections were ineffectual, they succeeded in delaying the completion of the sale until after midnight, and Hallett observed, "it is Sabbath day now, and it will not be legal to do it any how." Massachusetts law did indeed forbid this type of commercial transaction on Sundays. Thus, Loring turned to a deeply disappointed Grimes and said, "It can be done at eight o'clock on Monday morning — come to my office then, and it can be settled in five minutes."

Despite this setback, the conservative *Boston Advertiser* optimistically predicted that the sale would be consummated on Monday morning. Meanwhile, with the courthouse square still filled with thousands of onlookers, abolitionists and their allies sought to use the situation to further galvanize public opinion against the rendition proceedings. On Sunday a handbill was distributed proclaiming: "THE MAN IS NOT BOUGHT! HE IS STILL IN THE SLAVE PEN IN THE COURT HOUSE." The handbill went on to allege that Suttle had willfully broken the agreement to sell Burns and that the effort to recover Burns had been deliberately contrived to offend the sensibilities of antislavery Northerners and celebrate the passage of the Kansas-Nebraska Act.

The same day, at the Boston Music Hall, Theodore Parker delivered an extraordinary sermon that dealt at length with the killing of Batchelder and the arrests that followed. Suggesting that Batchelder might well have been killed accidentally by his fellow guards, Parker showed little sympathy for the dead man, asserting, "he liked the business of enslaving a man, and has gone to render an account to God for his gratuitous work." After observing that "one man is butchered, and twelve men [arrested and] brought in peril of their lives," Parker asked: "Why is this? Whose fault is it?" In assessing blame, Parker focused on an unlikely candidate: Edward Loring.

Paradoxically, Parker began his assault on Loring with a detailed catalog of Loring's personal virtues, describing the probate judge as "uniformly beloved," "a *respectable* man — in the Boston sense of that word, and in a much higher sense," and "a kind-hearted, charitable man; a good neighbor; a fast friend — when politics did not interfere; charitable with his purse; an excellent husband; a kind father; a good relative." And he expressed the hope that Loring "may yet act like a man." But Parker then proceeded to excoriate Loring's actions in the Burns case in the most inflammatory language imaginable:

> But, my friends, all this confusion is [Loring's] work. He knew he was *stealing a man*, born with the same right to life, liberty and the pursuit of happiness as himself. He knew the slaveholders had no more right to Anthony Burns than to his own daughter. He knew the consequences of stealing a man in Boston. He knew that there are men in Boston who have not yet conquered their prejudices — men who respect the higher law of God. He knew there would be a meeting at Faneuil Hall — gatherings in the street. He knew there would be violence.
>
> Edward Greely Loring . . . before these citizens of Boston, on Ascension Sunday, assembled to worship God, I charge you with the death of that man who was murdered on last Friday night. He was your fellow servant in kidnapping. He dies at your hand. You fired the shot that makes his wife a widow, his child an orphan. I charge you with the peril of twelve men, arrested for murder and on trial for their lives. I charge you with filling the Court House with one hundred and eighty-four hired ruffians of the United States, and alarming not only this city for her liberties that are in peril, but stirring up the whole Commonwealth of Massachusetts with indignation, which no man knows how to stop, which no man can stop. You have done it all!

Parker was not alone in condemning Loring's role in the Burns case. Loring was also privately urged to resign as a commissioner by

Harvard overseer John Gorham Palfrey, a leader of the Massachusetts Free-Soil Party and erstwhile Conscience Whig who had been instrumental in helping Loring secure his appointment to the Harvard faculty. Palfrey contended that because of Loring's faculty position and ongoing service as a state probate judge, his continued participation in the case might do institutional damage to both Harvard and the state judiciary generally. Palfrey asserted that if Loring felt compelled to continue to act as a commissioner enforcing the Fugitive Slave Act, he should resign both his probate judgeship and his faculty position at Harvard "so as not to impair vast interests by [his] actions [as a commissioner]." Against this background, Loring was no doubt anxious to have the entire problem resolved by the consummation of the agreement that had been reached on Saturday.

With the status of the agreement for sale far from clear, the continuing tension was fed by rumors that unnamed members of the Pierce administration were sending dispatches demanding that Burns be sent back to Virginia. Worried that on Monday morning Suttle would no longer be willing to accept the $1,200 for Burns's freedom, the Reverend Grimes arrived at Loring's home at 11 PM on Sunday and expressed his concern. Loring told Grimes that he believed Suttle was still willing to sell Burns and that if the sale was not consummated, Loring would give Burns the benefit of any doubts raised in the rendition proceeding. They once again agreed that Grimes should bring the payment to Loring's office at 8 AM on Monday.

But by Monday morning, Suttle had decided to pursue the rendition process to its conclusion. The reasons for his change of heart have never been definitively established. Some believe that Suttle was following the advice of Henry Watkins Allen, a Louisiana attorney Suttle had originally consulted about setting a price for Burns. On Sunday morning, Allen became aware of the Massachusetts statute barring the sale of slaves in the state. Unlike Loring, Allen was unwilling to definitively conclude that the transaction for Burns's freedom was not covered by that statute. Moreover, as Allen pointed out, the abolitionists had already charged Suttle with kidnapping Burns, who was described in the complaint as a "free citizen of Massachusetts," and there was no guarantee that they would not continue to use the antislavery statute to harass Suttle. Edward Parker, in contrast, claimed that the agreement to sell Burns collapsed because a $400 pledge toward the $1,200 sale price was conditioned on the transaction's consummation on Saturday night.

For whatever reason, by Monday morning, the agreement to free Burns by purchase was clearly off the table. When Grimes arrived at Loring's office at eight o'clock, he found it empty. After waiting until nine o'clock, Grimes went to Revere House in a vain effort to locate Suttle. Visits to Seth Thomas's office, back to Loring's office, and then to the probate court proved equally futile. Finally, Grimes discovered Suttle at Freeman's office, where Suttle was in conference with Freeman, Brent, Thomas, and Hallett. Suttle refused Grimes's offer to buy Burns, declaring that because the transaction had not been consummated on Saturday, he was absolved from the agreement. Suttle then stated, "when I get [Burns] back to Virginia, then you can buy him." Hallett volunteered to contribute $100 to the purchase price after Burns had been returned to Virginia. Thus, the effort to avoid the completion of the rendition proceeding had failed.

The Rendition Hearing

Against this background, with thousands of people still in the courthouse square and with access to the courthouse itself limited by hundreds of military personnel, the hearing reconvened before a packed courtroom at eleven o'clock that morning. The session began with a heated exchange between Charles Ellis and Benjamin Hallett over the show of force. Ellis complained about the atmosphere in which the proceedings were being conducted. After first asserting incorrectly that Burns was in shackles, Ellis noted that the courtroom "has been *packed* with armed men" and decried the presence of military men throughout the courthouse, which, he claimed, made it difficult for Burns's supporters to gain access to the hearing. Ellis asserted that "the object seems to be, for some cause, that the countenances about, instead of reflecting the benignity that ought to be shed from a tribunal of justice, only stare upon it with hate." Loring brushed aside these comments and ordered the hearing to proceed, though averring, "I will give this consideration if necessary, hereafter."

Hallett, however, was not satisfied with this calm response. He rose from his seat to take issue with Ellis's comments, declaring that "as the law officer of the United States and counsel for the United States marshal," he felt bound to defend the show of force. Brushing aside repeated efforts by Loring to deter him from speaking, Hallett noted that the military had been summoned pursuant to the order of Peleg Sprague and with the approval of President Pierce in response to the violence of the previous Friday evening, which Hallett blamed on "the conduct of men who got up and inflamed the meeting at Faneuil Hall, some of whom [Hallett] saw [in the courtroom] and some of who[m] were claimed by [Ellis] as his friends." Ellis began to object to the tone of Hallett's comments, but Loring silenced him, asserting that this "was a matter in which [Ellis] alone was interested." Loring then rejected Ellis's motion for a further delay of the proceedings. William Brent was called as a witness for the claimant. Brent gave a detailed description of Burns and stated that he had known Burns for a number of years. Brent testified that, acting as an agent for Suttle, he had hired Burns out, with the wages being paid to Suttle rather than Burns, and in March 1854, Millspaugh had been Burns's employer. Brent also stated that he had last seen Burns in Richmond on March 20. Thomas then sought to elicit an account of the May 24 conversation between Burns and Suttle.

Ellis and Dana quickly objected, contending that the introduction of these remarks was barred by section 6 of the Fugitive Slave Act, which provided that the testimony of the alleged fugitive should not be admitted into evidence in a rendition proceeding. In response, Thomas argued that the term *testimony* did not refer to confessions or admissions made outside the courtroom. Loring tentatively agreed with this conclusion and allowed Brent to proceed, but he left open the possibility that he might reverse this ruling later.

Brent then recounted the substance of Burns's statements, and this account was corroborated by Caleb Page, a teamster who had overheard the conversation. Finally, once again over Ellis's objection, Thomas introduced the record of the Alexandria circuit court to demonstrate that Burns had in fact been enslaved to Suttle and had escaped. At approximately 2:50 PM, the attorneys for Suttle ended their presentation. Ellis and Dana then asked for a delay, and Loring announced that the hearing would reconvene at 3:30.

When the hearing resumed, Charles Ellis began his opening argument for the defense. At the outset, Ellis once again challenged the notion that the rendition hearing was simply a preliminary step in the process of resolving Burns's legal status. Instead, Ellis contended that the hearing was the only meaningful legal process Burns was likely to receive, reiterating, "if you send [Burns] hence with [Suttle], he goes to the block, to the sugar or cotton plantation [and] to the lash." Thus, Ellis contended that the certificate of removal should not be issued "unless a case of overwhelming proof is presented, unless by no possibility could any but the slave of Suttle be seized or surrendered."

Against this background, Ellis announced that the defense would produce evidence showing that Burns had been a freeman in Boston prior to the time he allegedly escaped from Norfolk. Ellis then turned his attention to the certificate that had been issued by the Virginia court, which, he asserted, did not meet the requirements outlined in section 10 of the Fugitive Slave Act. In any event, Congress could not make such a certificate evidence of Burns's status.

In making this claim, Ellis was forced to confront not only arguments based on congressional power to enforce the Fugitive Slave Clause itself but also the contention that Congress was empowered to adopt section 10 by article IV, section 1, of the Constitution. Known as the Full Faith and Credit Clause, that section provides that "full faith and credit shall be given in each state to the public acts, records and judicial proceedings of every other state" and that "Congress may by general laws prescribe the manner in which such acts, records and proceedings shall be proved, and the effect thereof." Ellis asserted that the effect given to the certificate could not be justified by this provision for two reasons: first, the certificate did not constitute a judicial record within the meaning of the clause; and second, under the Constitution, the scope of the certificate's authority had to be determined by the law of Virginia, and under Virginia law, issuance of the certificate could not be used against Burns because he had not been given notice of the Virginia proceeding. At this point, with the clock reading 6 PM, Loring adjourned for the day.

Prior to the hearing's resumption, another effort was made to purchase Burns's freedom. On Tuesday morning Hamilton Willis, a State Street broker, approached Suttle in the marshal's office as a representative of "some of [Boston's] most respectable citizens [who] sought an adjustment of this unpleasant case." Explicitly recognizing Suttle's claim to Burns, Willis stated that a number of "highly esteemed citizens" had pledged whatever funds were necessary to purchase Burns's freedom. Suttle replied that he "wanted to see the result of the trial at any rate," and Willis apparently agreed to allow the rendition hearing to proceed to its conclusion and to compensate Suttle, whatever the result. Suttle then agreed to sell Burns with certain stipulations, purportedly for $4,000. Although not entirely happy with the stipulations, Willis agreed to the conditions.

However, before the agreement could be reduced to writing, Benjamin Hallett appeared at the marshal's office and took Suttle aside for a private conversation, after which Suttle told Willis, "I must withdraw what I have done with you." When Willis pressed Hallett to explain his opposition to the arrangement, Hallett pointed to the spot in the marshal's office where James Batchelder had collapsed and proclaimed, "that blood must be avenged."

Despite the failure of Willis's mission, by the time the proceeding reconvened on Tuesday morning at 9:30, the public excitement surrounding the case appeared to have lessened somewhat. The size of the crowd in the square was estimated as in the hundreds rather than the thousands, and the courtroom itself was less crowded than it had been the day before. Ellis, however, had lost none of his zeal for the defense of his client. Resuming his presentation, he argued that the warrant and complaint that gave rise to the rendition hearing were defective because they failed to allege a number of crucial facts with sufficient specificity. In addition, Ellis challenged the admissibility of the statements made by Burns when first confronted by Suttle, noting that, under common law, admissions by a putative slave in a trial for freedom were inadmissible and that section 6 of the Fugitive Slave Act explicitly prohibited alleged fugitives from testifying.

Ellis also asserted that, even if the two disputed pieces of evidence were admitted, Suttle had failed to prove his case. Ellis argued that since Burns had been hired out to Millspaugh at the time of the alleged escape, he was in essence leased property, and Suttle had no standing to bring legal proceedings to recover the services of the putative slave. In addition, Ellis contended that Loring could issue the certificate of removal only if Burns had consciously intended to escape, and the sole evidence on this point was Burns's own statement that he had inadvertently fallen asleep on the ship that had transported him to Boston.

Ellis concluded his argument by launching a full-bore attack on the constitutionality of the Fugitive Slave Act itself. He marshaled many of the standard antislavery arguments against the statute, most of which had been explicitly rejected by the *Sims* court. Ellis asserted that Congress lacked the power to adopt a fugitive slave statute; that the 1850 statute unconstitutionally vested the Virginia courts with federal judicial power; that commissioners such as Loring were also vested with judicial power, in violation of article III; and that the statute unconstitutionally denied jury trials to alleged fugitives and violated the search and seizure provisions of the Fourth Amendment and the Due Process Clause of the Fifth Amendment.

With its opening argument concluded, the defense called a series of witnesses whose testimony was designed to show that Burns could not be the man described in the Virginia transcript and Brent's testimony. The first of these witnesses was William Jones, a free African American laborer. On direct examination from Ellis and cross-examination from Suttle's lawyers, Jones gave a detailed account of his relationship with Burns. Jones testified that he met Burns on March 1 — more than two weeks before Brent claimed to have last seen the missing slave in Virginia — when Burns approached Jones in the street and asked if he knew of any stores where he might find work. According to Jones, the two men were companions from March 1 through March 18.

Jones stated that, after unsuccessfully seeking employment at City Hall on March 3, he obtained employment at the Mattapan Iron Works on March 4 and subsequently employed Burns for five days to help him clean windows there, paying Burns eight cents per window for a total of $1.50. To confirm this recollection, Jones produced a memorandum book in which the transaction had been recorded. Jones further stated that he and Burns worked together at City Hall on March 18 and then parted company. Jones did not see Burns again prior to his arrest on May 24.

The remainder of Jones's testimony was somewhat disjointed. He stated that he had first heard of Burns's arrest on Thursday, May 25, and had actually seen his face through a courthouse window on Sunday, had attended the Faneuil Hall meeting and gone to the courthouse with the crowd, had attempted to see Suttle at Revere House, and had tried unsuccessfully to attend the hearing on Saturday. Jones also asserted that he had applied for a permit to visit Burns in person but had been rebuffed by Freeman.

Given his rambling presentation and considered alone, Jones's testimony might not have been particularly persuasive. Indeed, when Jones first took the stand, Benjamin Hallett muttered, "here comes a witness that [Theodore] Parker has got to perjure himself." But Ellis quickly produced two other witnesses — both white — who corroborated the critical details of Jones's account. George W. Drew, bookkeeper at the Mattapan Iron Works at the time, testified that Burns had in fact been employed as a window washer there in early March and had at one point come to Drew to ask how much Jones had been paid for the work. Drew said he had confirmed the date by referring to the entry book in the company ledger that documented the payment for the work. James Whittemore, a member of the City Council who had been a machinist at the same company, remembered seeing Burns there. Whittemore also volunteered, pointedly, that he was not a "Free Soiler or Abolitionist" and described himself as a "hunker Whig." The defense called six other witnesses, each of whom recalled seeing Burns in Boston in early March.

In rebuttal, Suttle's attorneys first called Cyrus Gould, the custodian of City Hall, who testified that Jones had worked there on several occasions in March, but Gould had never seen Burns with him. Another witness was called, but his testimony was disallowed after objection from the defense. Loring then adjourned the hearing for the day.

By the time the hearing reconvened the following morning, the size of the crowd and the general level of excitement in the square had diminished even further. Nonetheless, as a precaution against any more incendiary meetings, both Faneuil Hall and the Music Hall were ordered closed by the city government. The session began with three more rebuttal witnesses from the claimant. The testimony of two of those witnesses proved to be inconsequential. Erastus B. Gould, a worker at the city building, averred that he had hired Jones to work at the building on March 26 but had never seen Burns with Jones. William R. Batchelder (who may have been related to the man killed in the attempt to free Burns) sought to testify about a conversation he had had with Jones outside the courthouse, but based on an objection from the defense, his testimony was excluded.

The last witness was Benjamin True, a guard from the marshal's office who had stayed in the jury room with Burns since his arrest. True's testimony was intended to prove that Burns had admitted not arriving in Boston until March 19. Dana objected on the ground that such testimony was not proper rebuttal, but Loring overruled the objection. True then testified that Burns had stated he had been in Boston "about two months, or a little short of that," and that prior to coming to Boston he had been in Richmond.

After the completion of True's testimony, Richard Henry Dana began the closing argument for the defense. After congratulating Loring for nearing the end of his "anxious and painful" labors, Dana launched a series of sarcastic attacks on those who had supported the claimant and garrisoned the courthouse. He congratulated the state of Massachusetts "that at length, in due time, by leave of the Marshal of the United States and the District Attorney of the United States . . . her courts may be reopened and her judges, suitors and witnesses may pass and repass without being obliged to satisfy hirelings of the United States Marshal and bayoneted foreigners, that they have a right to be there." Dana then turned his fire on Benjamin Hallett, congratulating the federal government "that its legal representative can return to his appropriate duties, and that his sedulous presence will no longer be needed here in a private civil suit for the purpose of intimidation, a purpose which his [outburst on May 29] showed every desire to effect." Dana also rebuked Loring for not taking stronger action against Hallett during and after the outburst. Finally, Dana congratulated "the officers of the army and navy, that they can be relieved of this service . . . and can draw off their non-commissioned officers and privates, both drunk and sober, from this fortified slave-pen, to the custody of the forts and fleets of our country, which have been left in peril, that this great Republic might add to its glories the trophies of one more captured slave."

Having vented his displeasure at the actions taken by the representatives of the federal government, Dana launched into his arguments regarding the issues raised by the legal proceedings in the Burns case. He began by reiterating Ellis's contention that the claimant was required to prove all the relevant factual points beyond a reasonable doubt. In support of the position, Dana cited Sir Matthew Hale's observation that "it was better that nine guilty men should escape than that one innocent man should suffer" and noted that this principle was universally applied in cases of murder, "where one man's life was on one side and the interest of an entire community on the other." Dana argued that application of that principle was even more apt in a case involving slavery. He described the interest of the alleged slave as "more sacred than life," asserting, "here is a question of a few despised pieces of silver on the one hand, and on the other the perpetual bondage of a man, from early manhood to an early or late grave, and the bondage of the fruit of his body forever." He once again emphasized what he saw as the likely fate of Burns if Suttle prevailed, stating, "the man you send away would be sold. He would never see the Virginia sun. He would be sold at the first block, to perish after a few years of unwonted service, on the cotton fields or sugar fields of Louisiana and Arkansas."

The argument then turned to the evidence of Burns's identity. Dana contended that the description of the escapee in the transcript from the Virginia court was vague at best, observing that the severe damage to Burns's right hand was described as only a "scar." In addition, noting that Brent had characterized the injury as only a "cut," Dana found it "extraordinary" that neither the transcript not Brent's testimony had given a more fulsome description of "the most noticeable part" of Burns's appearance, and also pointed out that Brent had described the large brand on Burns's cheek as simply a "scar."

Dana hypothesized two explanations for the lack of specificity in Brent's testimony, neither of which was favorable to Suttle. One possibility was that Brent did not know Burns well, in which case the identification was inherently unreliable. Alternatively, Dana suggested darkly that Brent's testimony might have been influenced by a desire to satisfy the pro-slavery establishment in Virginia, implicitly suggesting to Loring that the commissioner would inevitably be required to choose a side in the sectional conflict:

Remember . . . the state of political excitement at this moment. Remember the state of feeling between North and South; the contest between the slave power and the free power. Remember that this case is made a state issue by Virginia, a national question by the Executive. Reflect that every reading man in Virginia, with all the pride of the Old Dominion aroused in him, is turning his eyes, is turning his eyes to the result of this issue. No man could be more liable to bias than a Virginian, testifying in Massachusetts at this moment, on such an issue, with every powerful and controlling motive on earth enlisted for success.

The defense argument then turned to the most explicit aspect of Brent's testimony: the assertion that Brent had seen the escapee in Richmond on March 20 and that the escape had taken place between that date and March 24. After providing a detailed summary of the testimony of the parade of witnesses who placed Burns in Boston well before March 20, Dana argued that this testimony demonstrated conclusively that Burns could not be the escaped slave Brent had described.

But Dana was not content to rest his defense on the issue of identity. He also contended that Suttle's attorneys had failed to prove that Burns owed service to Suttle and that Burns had in fact escaped. On these points, Dana was initially confronted with the problem of evading the evidentiary rule established by section 10. Although section 10 explicitly provides for "production [by the claimant] of other and further evidence if necessary, either oral or by affidavit, in addition to what is contained in the . . . record [of the state court]," Dana contended that the modes of proceeding established by section 10 and section 6, respectively, were mutually exclusive and that, by calling Brent as a witness, Suttle had elected to proceed under section 6. Like Ellis before him, Dana also asserted that, in any event, Suttle could not take advantage of the provisions of section 10 because of technical flaws in the Virginia record. Treating the issues of service and escape as open questions, Dana's argument followed much the same pattern as Ellis's opening statement. Dana reiterated that the only evidence bearing on the issue of escape was Burns's own statement that he had accidentally fallen asleep on the ship and argued vigorously that only Millspaugh had standing to initiate an action under the Fugitive Slave Act. Dana also made much of the fact that Millspaugh had never been called to testify to Burns's identity.

The defense argument then turned to the damaging statements Burns had made to Suttle during their initial encounter at the courthouse. Dana expressed regret that Loring had not ruled the statements inadmissible, contending that such a ruling would have been more consistent with "reason, humanity, and precedent," and he asserted that the circumstances under which the statements had been made "deprive[d them] of all weight" as evidence. Dana reminded Loring of Burns's "stupefied and terrified condition" at the time of the confrontation with Suttle and noted that Benjamin True — a witness for the claimant — had described Burns as "intimidated" by his situation. Dana then concluded his argument by once again reminding Loring of both the consequences for Burns of a ruling in favor of Suttle and the prominence the case had assumed in the sectional conflict:

{ *Chapter 5* }

You recognized, Sir, in the beginning, the presumption of freedom. Hold to it now, Sir, as to the sheet-anchor of your peace of mind as well as of [Burns's] safety. If you commit a mistake in favor of the man, a pecuniary value, not great, is put at hazard. If against him, a free man is made a slave forever. If you have, on the evidence or on the law, the doubt of a reasoning and reasonable mind, an intelligent misgiving, then, Sir, I implore you, in view of the cruel character of this law, in view of the dreadful consequences of a mistake, send him not away, with that tormenting doubt on your mind. It may turn to a torturing certainty. The eyes of millions are upon you, Sir. You are to do an act which will hold its place in the history of America, in the history of the progress of the human race. May your judgment be for liberty and not for slavery, for happiness and not for wretchedness; for hope and not for despair.

Seth Thomas then closed for the claimant. He too began with a series of congratulations, but not surprisingly, his tone was far different from Dana's. Thomas congratulated all those involved in the presentation of the case and the defense of the courthouse because "they were about to be relieved from a service on which they had entered, not as volunteers, but from a sense of duty, and from which they could all retire with a consciousness that the blood of the murdered man did not at least rest with them." In particular, he praised Marshal Freeman for his "firmness, decision, prudence, and kindness to the defendant" in the performance of an "arduous" duty, and he praised Loring for showing "equal justice and liberality to either side." Finally, directly challenging the tactics of the radical abolitionists in general and Theodore Parker (who was present at the hearing) in particular, Thomas congratulated the city of Boston "that order was supreme; that Faneuil Hall, cradle of law as well as liberty, was closed today against treasonable and insane speech; and that the Music Hall, too, was closed against blasphemy of Almighty God, and to charges of murder done by this court—made by one . . . who, though not a lawyer, but claiming to be a minister of the gospel, has the assurance to come here within the bar and occupy a privileged seat."

Turning to the body of his argument, Thomas began by claiming that under section 10, the questions of whether Burns owed service to Suttle and had escaped were foreclosed by the Virginia transcript, and the adoption of section 10 was itself a constitutional exercise of the authority granted by the Full Faith and Credit Clause. Beginning from this premise, Thomas focused most of his attention on the question of whether the African American man in the courtroom was in fact the Anthony Burns named in the transcript.

Thomas emphasized that, as specified in the certificate and described by Brent, Burns was in fact a man of the appropriate age who was six feet tall with a dark complexion and scars on both his right hand and his cheek. Thomas observed that "it would be difficult to find another colored person in the whole of Boston who so well answers the description as the person at the bar." Addressing the question of when Burns came to Boston, Thomas contended that Jones, aided and abetted by one of the other African American witnesses, had manufactured the story about working with Burns in early March. Thomas further suggested that Jones had gone to the other supporting witnesses and told them that the black man they had seen him working with had been Burns, and this suggestion led those witnesses to identify Burns in the courtroom.

But, Thomas contended, even if the alibi testimony was believed, it was not fatal to the claimant's case. At most, he argued, the testimony suggested that Brent was mistaken about the date of Burns's escape, and that date was irrelevant to the question of whether Burns was in fact a fugitive slave. Thomas further observed that if Burns had not escaped from Richmond, the defense would have identified the city where he had lived before coming to Boston, rather than vaguely asserting that Burns "may have come from New York or Cincinnati or Canada." The defense had suggested that Burns may have refused to specify his city of origin for fear of endangering relatives there, who might themselves be fugitive slaves. Thomas observed, however, that any such danger could have been minimized by simply notifying the relatives before the city was identified.

After completing his analysis of the identity issue, Thomas discussed the basic nature of the proceedings. He took sharp issue with the claim that the rendition proceeding was, in essence, a final determination of Burns's status. Instead, he noted that Loring was only being asked to send Burns to Virginia. At that point, Thomas observed, the responsibility shifted to the government of Virginia, cavalierly asserting, "if the laws of that state don't sufficiently guard his rights, the responsibility is not yours or mine." But at the same time, Thomas noted that the laws of Virginia did allow Burns to pursue an action for his freedom in state court. He then summarily dismissed the challenge to the constitutionality of the Fugitive Slave Act more generally, asserting that, with the exception of section 10, the statute was in all important respects similar to the 1793 law that had been upheld in *Prigg*, and in any event, the 1850 statute itself had been upheld by every court that had heard the issue.

At this point, claiming that he had several more points to make, Thomas asked for leave to continue his argument on Thursday. However, Loring denied this request, citing both his desire to bring the case to a conclusion and the fact that the circuit court would be using the courtroom the next day. Thus, Thomas quickly brought his argument to a close, decrying the "extraordinary bitterness" that had marked the presentations of Burns's attorneys and reaffirming the basic points of the claimant's case. Loring then adjourned the proceedings until Friday morning at nine o'clock, when it was generally expected that a decision would be rendered.

CHAPTER 6

The Verdict

Some of the opponents of the Fugitive Slave Act were hopeful that Loring would set Burns free. But it was also widely rumored that in the event of a ruling against the claimant, Suttle and his allies would seize Burns by force and carry him off to Virginia or, in the alternative, the putative slave would simply be rearrested and brought before another rendition tribunal. Indeed, Suttle had written a letter asserting that he would "never break the hold [on Burns] which law and right give him." Meanwhile, the Vigilance Committee continued to weigh a variety of options that might be pursued in the event Loring ruled in favor of Suttle.

The federal authorities were also making preparations for a potential verdict against Burns. On May 30 Marshal Freeman notified Mayor Smith that, in Freeman's view, the forces currently deployed were insufficient to guarantee order, and "if bloodshed is to be prevented in the public streets, there must be such a demonstration of a military force as will overawe attack." Freeman asked Smith to place the volunteer militia at the disposal of Major General Benjamin F. Edmands of the state militia to provide such a force. In addition, at the behest of President Pierce, Secretary of War Jefferson Davis ordered Colonel Samuel Cooper, the adjutant general of the army, to go to Boston and provide the military force required to keep order and, if necessary, effectuate the rendition of Burns.

Smith apparently balked at the cost of mobilizing the militia, and the following day, President Pierce ordered Hallett "to incur any expenses necessary" to ensure the execution of the Fugitive Slave Act. Freeman and Hallett then informed Smith that, if Burns was remanded to Suttle's custody and had to be transported through Boston, "the whole military and police force of the city [would be required] to preserve the peace of the city and prevent riot and assaults upon the officers of the law in the discharge of their duty," and the federal government would take responsibility for the cost. However, understanding that the Latimer law prohibited state and local officials from participating in the rendition of fugitive slaves, Freeman and Hallett emphasized that the militia would not participate in the rendition process per se, but only keep order as federal troops transported Burns through the city.

Thursday was a day of nervous anticipation for all those with interests in the Burns case. That afternoon Freeman visited Loring in the hope of obtaining advance notice of the decision, to allow him to make the appropriate security arrangements. Both Freeman and Richard Henry Dana would later insist that Loring refused to reveal his decision to Freeman; however, at 9:15 PM, a man named John W. Way visited Charles Ellis and told him that, according to Freeman, Burns would be sent back to Virginia.

Even if the authorities were uncertain about Loring's decision, the prudent course of action was to prepare for the unrest that was likely to ensue in the event Suttle prevailed in the rendition proceeding. Accordingly, on Thursday evening, there was a meeting in the mayor's office that was attended by Freeman; Hallett; Edmands; Major Dulany, who commanded the marines stationed at Charlestown; and Peter Dunbar, a customhouse official who had recruited the civilians guarding the courthouse under Freeman's command. Mindful of the constraints imposed by the Latimer law, Edmands refused to allow the local militia to be used as an escort to help bring Burns from the courthouse to the ship waiting to transport him and Suttle to Virginia. However, Edmands did affirm that Mayor Smith could use the troops "for the purpose of aiding the civil authorities in keeping the peace of the city."

As partisans of all stripes anxiously awaited Loring's decision, tensions rose to a fever pitch. On Friday morning, thousands of Bostonians thronged the courthouse square. A company of U.S. Infantry armed with an artillery piece guarded the main entrance to the courthouse itself, and Freeman arranged to have the courtroom where the decision would be read crowded with armed civilian guards. Mayor Smith issued a proclamation warning that Major General Edmands and the chief of police had forces under their command stationed throughout the city and that these forces were "clothed with full discretionary powers to sustain the laws of the land." Smith called on "all well-disposed citizens and other persons . . . to leave those streets which it may be found necessary to clear temporarily, and under no circumstances to molest any officer, civil or military, in the lawful discharge of their duties."

Against this background, half a dozen guards escorted Burns into the courtroom at 8:45. Loring took his seat fifteen minutes later. The attorneys for both sides soon followed, as did a number of members of the Vigilance Committee, including Wendell Phillips and Theodore Parker. Suttle and Brent did not attend the proceedings; they had checked out of Revere House early that morning and were awaiting word of the decision on the U.S. revenue cutter *Morris*, which had been dispatched to Boston to facilitate the potential rendition of Burns.

Loring began to read his decision shortly after 9 AM. The first course of business was a discussion of the constitutional objections raised by the defense attorneys. Rather than accepting the defense's view that the rendition proceeding was, in effect, a final determination of Burns's status, Loring — like Story before him — took the position that the Fugitive Slave Act was nothing more than an extradition statute that required the commissioner to perform a simple "ministerial" act. Thus, Loring rejected the argument that a jury trial was required by the Constitution, observing that the statute "gives to the fugitive from service a much better protection than a fugitive from justice can claim from the law." The same conception of his function underlay Loring's treatment of the assertion that the statute unconstitutionally delegated federal judicial power to officials who did not meet the standards of article III judges. He observed that, in other contexts, federal law granted similar powers to both commissioners of the court of claims and local magistrates, and if the Fugitive Slave Act was unconstitutional on this ground, then so were these widely accepted delegations of power by Congress. He gave similarly short shrift to the argument that section 10 was unconstitutional, asserting that the provision giving conclusive authority to the transcript from the Virginia court was a legitimate exercise of the power granted to Congress by the Full Faith and Credit Clause.

Loring did not discuss the remaining constitutional objections individually, observing that they had already been rejected by a variety of state and federal courts. He focused primarily on the opinion in *Sims*, noting that the Massachusetts Supreme Court had upheld the constitutionality of the Fugitive Slave Act after "the fullest argument and maturest deliberation." Loring then quoted at length Chief Justice Shaw's elaboration of the Hunker Whig view of the Fugitive Slave Clause:

> Slavery was not created, established, or perpetuated, by the Constitution; it existed before; it would have existed if the Constitution had not been made. The framers of the Constitution could not abrogate slavery, or the rights claimed under it. They took it as they found it, and regulated it to a limited extent. The Constitution, therefore, is not responsible for the origin or continuance of slavery; the provision it contains was the best adjustment which could be made of conflicting rights and claims, and was absolutely necessary to effect what may now be considered as the general pacification, by which harmony and peace should take the place of violence and war. These were the circumstances, and this the spirit, in which the Constitution was made; the regulation of slavery, so far as to prohibit States by law from harboring fugitive slaves, was an essential element in its formation, and the Union intended to be established by it was essentially necessary to the peace, happiness, and highest prosperity of all the States. In this spirit, and with these views steadily in prospect, it seems to be the duty of all judges and magistrates to expound and apply these provisions in the Constitution and laws of the United States, and in this spirit it behooves all persons bound to obey the laws of the United States, to consider and regard them.

At this point, Loring chose to respond publicly to those who had urged him to refuse to participate in the rendition hearing because the Fugitive Slave Act was fundamentally immoral. After noting that it was not the function of the judiciary to determine whether a constitutional law was "wicked and cruel," he argued that it was the duty of good men to participate in rendition proceedings to ameliorate the harshness of the statute itself:

> It is said that the statute is so cruel and wicked that it should not be executed by good men. Then into what hands shall its administra-

tion fall, and in its administration, what is to be the protection of the unfortunate men who are brought within its operation? Will those who call the statute merciless, commit it to a merciless judge? If the statute involves that right, which for us makes life sweet, and the want of which makes life a misfortune, shall its administration be confined to those who are reckless of that right to others, or ignorant or careless of the means given for its legal defence, or dishonest in their use? If any men wish this, they are more cruel and wicked than the statute, for they would strip from the fugitive the best security and every alleviation the statute leaves him.

In any event, under Loring's view of the case, the only question remaining to be decided was whether the man before him was the Anthony Burns described in the Virginia transcript. Loring reviewed the conflicting testimony of William Brent and the defense witnesses. Loring brushed aside the attorneys' efforts to impugn the motives of opposing witnesses. He declared that although Brent was "standing in circumstances that would bias the fairest mind . . . other imputation than this has not been offered against him, and from any thing that has appeared before me, cannot be." Conversely, Loring also asserted that "the [defense] testimony is from many witnesses whose integrity is admitted, and to whom no imputation of bias can be attached by the evidence in the case." In addition, he described the source of the knowledge of all the identity witnesses as personal and direct, but he viewed the testimony of the defense witnesses as "less full and complete" than that of Brent.

Faced with what he viewed as a "complete and irreconcilable" conflict between facially credible witnesses, Loring turned to the statements of the "one person whose knowledge is perfect and positive, and whose evidence is not within the reach of error": Burns himself. Loring relied heavily on Suttle's uncontradicted, corroborated characterization of the exchange with Burns at the courthouse, focusing particularly on the fact that Burns had greeted Suttle and Brent using their first names. Though conceding that Burns's statements regarding the details of his service to Suttle might be discounted because they were "in the nature of admissions [by] a man stupefied by circumstances and fear," Loring found no evidence that the greetings themselves had been influenced or procured by "hope or fear." Thus, as Burns silently mouthed the word "no," Loring concluded that Suttle had proved beyond a reasonable doubt that Burns was in fact the man described in the Virginia transcript and ordered him returned to Suttle's service.

CHAPTER 7

Return to Bondage

The reactions to Loring's decision differed widely. Benjamin Hallett was, of course, extremely satisfied with this conclusion. He wired Franklin Pierce's personal secretary to inform him that "the Commissioner has granted the certificate. Fugitive will be removed to-day. Ample military and police force to effect it peacefully. All quiet. Law reigns."

Conversely, the antislavery forces were dismayed. By ten o'clock Loring had finished reading his decision and ordered the courtroom cleared. As they left, a number of Vigilance Committee members stopped briefly to offer their condolences to Burns. Leonard Grimes and Richard Henry Dana stayed behind to provide further support. Trying to lift Burns's spirits, Grimes told him that it had become a point of honor to have him returned and that Suttle would be willing to sell Burns as soon as he had been returned to Virginia. But Burns was pessimistic about his future; he expressed the fear that, once in Virginia, he would be forgotten by his Northern friends and sold south because of his injured hand. Indeed, fear of such a fate was the reason he had run away.

At eleven o'clock Burns was returned to his cell. Dana and Grimes stayed with him a few more minutes and promised Burns they would accompany him to the waiting ship. Freeman, however, vetoed this plan, so Grimes and Dana said their good-byes to Burns. They asked to speak to Burns in private, but this request was also refused. Grimes gave his address to Burns, and then he and Dana left. At the same time, Wendell Phillips arrived, and Burns asked whether there was anything more to be done. Phillips replied, "Burns, there isn't humanity, there isn't Christianity, there isn't justice enough here to save you."

In the city of Boston at large, the decision generated intense excitement. Although the courthouse square itself was cleared after Loring rendered his decision, every street leading to the square remained packed with people. A detachment of military personnel making its way to the courthouse was met with groans, hisses, and cries of "shame, shame," while Dana was cheered lustily as he left the building. A number of businesses were closed, and black banners hung from many windows. An American flag was displayed draped in black, and a coffin was suspended from a building near the courthouse with the inscription "The Funeral of Liberty."

But even in the wake of their disappointment with Loring's decision, the antislavery forces planned last-minute maneuvers designed to forestall Burns's return to Virginia. Hamilton Willis approached attorneys Thomas and Parker at the courthouse and offered to pay whatever Suttle might ask to purchase Burns's freedom, with Burns to be delivered either at Willis's State Street office or on board the *Morris*, whichever Suttle chose. Parker initially agreed to convey the offer to Suttle, and Willis obtained permission from Freeman to have the parties board the boat. But after consulting with Hallett, Parker stated that Suttle had made an unambiguous commitment not to sell Burns until after the fugitive had been returned to Virginia. Thus, the offer was summarily rejected. Frustrated, Willis approached a member of the Vigilance Committee and offered to provide a boat for a rescue effort. But by that time, any such effort would have been fruitless.

Last-ditch legal maneuvers proved to be equally impracticable. The Vigilance Committee had hoped to obtain a writ of personal replevin even after Loring's decision and to serve the writ forcibly on Suttle. But perhaps foreseeing that eventuality, Suttle took advantage of section 9 of the Fugitive Slave Act and, after Loring had issued the certificate, executed an affidavit declaring that Suttle "ha[d] reason to apprehend that [Burns] will be rescued by force," which triggered an obligation for the federal government to return Burns to Virginia, if necessary. Thus, Suttle was able to remain ensconced on the *Morris*, safely out of reach of any state legal process.

In the meantime, those charged with making the security arrangements for Burns's transfer were facing their own difficulties. Preparations were set back when Captain Joseph K. Hayes of the police department refused to participate in the implementation of these measures. Apparently unbeknownst to his superiors, Hayes was a member of the Vigilance Committee and had been acting as a spy for the antislavery forces, passing along details of the plan to transfer Burns in the event Suttle prevailed. At 11 AM on Friday he resigned his commission rather than participate in the transfer. In his written letter of resignation Hayes implied that, in his opinion, even providing general security would violate the Latimer law, declaring that he had "received an order which, if performed, would implicate me in the execution of that infamous 'Fugitive Slave Law.' "

Initially, Marshal Freeman planned to begin transferring Burns to the wharf at 12:30 PM, and by noon, military personnel had closed all the streets leading to the route along which Burns would be transported. But by early in the afternoon, Freeman still had not been informed of the status of the remaining security arrangements, and he summoned Edmands to ask about the situation. When Edmands informed him that some important points had been left unguarded by the police, Freeman sent Edmands to Mayor Smith, who immediately directed Edmands to fortify those positions.

By 2:30 all was in readiness, and as tens of thousands of people looked on, the actual process of moving Burns began. As he left the courthouse, Burns was surrounded by a heavily armed contingent of a "*hard* looking set of men . . . on a *hard* business." Leading the entourage was a detachment of the Boston Lancers, followed by a company of U.S. Army Infantry from Portsmouth, Maine, a company of U.S. marines, and a hollow square of approximately 100 U.S. marshals and their deputies, with Burns himself in the center of the square, resplendent in a new frock coat, silk vest, and blue silk handkerchief — going-away presents from his jailers. The square itself was flanked by another company of marines and followed by a detachment of artillery troops who attended a nine-pound artillery piece loaded with grapeshot. The entire Boston police force was also mobilized to minimize the risk of disorder at the periphery of the procession.

Spectators crammed every conceivable vantage point to get a glimpse of Burns and his entourage. Jeers and catcalls followed the procession as it wended its way through the streets of the city, and when the procession passed the offices of the antislavery *Commonwealth* newspaper, the military escort was showered with cayenne pepper, vitriol, and cowitch, a plant extract that can cause severe itching. William Jones, whose testimony had figured so prominently in the rendition hearing, was arrested at the wharf for using "exciting language." A number of others were arrested for minor offenses as well.

At one point the situation came close to erupting into a wide-ranging confrontation between the authorities and the onlookers. A horse was killed by one of the escorts after a delivery man refused to be deterred from attempting to cross the line of men surrounding Burns. The crowd surged against the military line, and an officer ordered the escort to fire on the crowd. However, the order was quickly countermanded, and the assault was repulsed without shots being fired. Thus, although a handful of people were badly injured in the excitement surrounding Burns's transfer, the entourage ultimately made its way through the streets of Boston without a major conflagration.

When Burns and his guards reached the wharf, he could not be transferred directly to the *Morris*. The original plan had been for the cutter to dock there, but at the last minute, permission had been denied by John H. Pearson, who controlled the wharf. Thus, Burns was first taken to the steamer *John Taylor*. At 3:20 he and his guards were transported to join Suttle and Brent on the *Morris*, which was lying near Fort Independence in Boston Harbor. Burns and six of his guards, including Asa Butman, then boarded the *Morris*, and the erstwhile fugitive began his journey back to Virginia.

Predictably, the resolution of the Burns case provoked a variety of reactions. For example, the abolitionist *Worcester Spy* declared, "the law of God, written in the people's hearts, and the law of man, written in the Constitution, were against the rendition of [Burns] to slavery; but the law of Virginia, sustained by the bayonets of the military . . . was in favor of it, and, of course, everything had to give way before the omnipotent edict of the Slave Power." In contrast, the *New York Journal of Commerce*, which was consistently sympathetic to the views of the Southern states, cheered "the complete triumph of law in Boston over one of the most ferocious gangs of Abolitionists . . . that ever disgraced the country." Blaming the expenditures incurred by the federal government on Burns's supporters, the same newspaper declared, "if it had been $300,000, the money would have been well-expended, rather than permit a law of the land, enacted to carry out a fundamental article of the national compact, to be trampled under foot." The *Journal*'s only complaint was that "Theodore Parker, Wendell Phillips, and other insurrectionist leaders [were not] taken into custody at the moment that their speeches gave the first occasion to the riot!" Similarly, in a public letter, H. W. Allen of Louisiana wrote, "the South will never forget this act of justice; and when I shall return to my own State, I can say to Louisianians that Boston is a law-abiding city, and that I have seen the rights of Southern men respected and firmly maintained."

However, many other Southerners were disturbed by the turmoil surrounding Burns's rendition. For example, the *Richmond Examiner* declared that "such an execution of the Fugitive Slave law as that which we witness in Boston is a mockery and an insult [and must] awaken the South to a sense of its position and the necessity of an independent and exclusive policy. . . . A few more such victories, and the South is undone." Some Bostonians seemed to be equally irate; on the evening of the rendition, Richard Henry Dana was mugged, apparently by two men who had been among the temporary guards hired to protect the courthouse from attempts to free Burns.

But in any event, the transfer of Burns to the *Morris* was not the end of the story. Despite Loring's decision, Burns would soon return to Boston as a freeman. Moreover, the controversy over Burns's rendition would not only have a significant impact on the lives of a number of principals in the drama but also influence the course of Massachusetts politics for years to come.

CHAPTER 8

The Fate of Anthony Burns

The party accompanying Anthony Burns on his journey south did not remain together for long. Charles Suttle and William Brent became seasick and left the *Morris* in New York. Burns then continued the voyage to Norfolk under the supervision of Asa Butman and his comrades. Burns and his guards arrived in Norfolk on June 10. He was kept in jail for two days, while his guards were treated to a dinner held in their honor. On June 12 the Burns party was transported to Richmond on the steamer *Jamestown*, where the guards were once again hailed at a dinner before returning to Boston.

Not surprisingly, Burns himself received far different treatment. He was immediately incarcerated in the Richmond city jail, where he remained for ten days. Burns was then transferred to the custody of Robert Lumpkin, a slave trader who operated a "trader's jail" on the outskirts of Richmond. This facility — a three-story brick structure surrounded by an acre of ground and a fence topped with iron spikes — was designed to house slaves brought to the city for sale, as well as slaves sent there by their masters for punishment.

At the same time, Leonard Grimes and Hamilton Willis were renewing their efforts to purchase Burns's freedom. At Grimes's instance, Willis sent a letter to Suttle to reopen negotiations, and Suttle replied on June 27, stating that he had "much difficulty in my own mind as to the course I ought [to] pursue about the [proposed] sale." On the one hand, the idea of a sale was flatly opposed by other slave owners because it might provide an incentive for other slaves to attempt to escape. On the other hand, Suttle professed to have "no little attachment" for Burns and "some disposition to see the experiment tried of bettering his condition." He also observed that the current offer was not being made by "abolitionists and incendiaries who put the laws of Union at defiance, and dyed their hands in the blood of Batchelder, but from those who struggled to maintain law and order."

After weighing these competing considerations, Suttle indicated that he would be willing to sell Burns, but he was no longer willing to accept the $1,200 agreed on in Boston. Instead, he now set the price at $1,500, observing that because of "the course pursued of violent, corrupt and opposition to [his] rights, [his] expenses were greatly increased."

Seeking to raise the additional $300, Grimes first approached Hallett, pointing out that he had been responsible for the collapse of the original agreement. Though reaffirming his offer to contribute $100 toward the purchase of Burns's freedom, Hallett refused to increase his contribution. The other potential donors took a similar view. In the wake of these developments, Thomas and Parker, who had represented Suttle in the proceedings, provided a letter stating that Suttle was obligated to sell Burns for $1,200, and Grimes wrote to Suttle to notify him that the offer would not exceed that price. But Suttle did not reply, and the effort to purchase the freedom of Anthony Burns failed once again.

Burns spent the next four months shackled hand and foot in an unsanitary cell no more than eight feet square. Communication between Burns and the other slaves housed at the jail was strictly forbidden, and for the first few weeks, Burns was given little food or water. His fetters were removed only once a day, when curiosity seekers who came to the jail were given an opportunity to see the famous escapee.

However, after Burns became ill, the conditions of his confinement were eased slightly. He was freed from his shackles more often and used the time to devise a makeshift communication system with other prisoners by using a spoon to enlarge a small hole in the floor of his cell. Burns also sought to communicate with the outside world, writing letters with ink and stationery he had secreted on his person at the time of his imprisonment and throwing the letters through the barred windows when he saw a black man passing by. Remarkably, one of the letters, dated August 23, actually reached Dana, but for whatever reason, the abolitionist lawyer apparently made no effort to improve Burns's situation.

Ultimately, Suttle decided to sell Burns, and in November the slave was placed on the auction block at a fair in Richmond. The feelings engendered by the conflict in Boston still ran high, and the crowd reacted loudly and angrily to Burns's appearance. At first, few were willing to bid on such a notorious ex-fugitive. However, Burns was ultimately sold for $905 to David McDaniel, a plantation owner and slave trader from Rocky Mount, North Carolina. To avoid further disturbances, McDaniel spirited Burns to the Richmond train station under cover of darkness, and from there, the two made the journey to the Rocky Mount plantation by train and private conveyance.

At Rocky Mount, Burns had charge of the horses and mules owned by McDaniel. Compared with slaves employed as field hands, Burns led a relatively privileged life during this period. Rather than living in the slave quarters, he had his own room in an office and took his meals at the master's house as well. Against McDaniel's express orders, Burns preached to the other slaves, but when he was discovered doing so on one occasion, McDaniel simply ignored the offense.

Burns continued to attempt to communicate with those who had supported him during his ordeal in Boston. Although most of these efforts were apparently fruitless, Dana did receive another letter shortly before Christmas that clearly indicated Burns was in Rocky Mount. Once again, however, Dana did not make any effort to arrange for the purchase of Burns's freedom.

Instead, the chain of events that would ultimately lead to the end of Burns's enslavement began with a chance encounter. One day, after driving McDaniel's wife to the home of a neighbor, Burns was identified to the neighbor as the slave whose rendition had caused such an uproar in Boston. A woman who was living in the neighbor's home recounted the incident in a letter to her sister in Amherst, Massachusetts, who in turn told the story at a social gathering where the Reverend G. S. Stockwell, a Baptist clergyman, was present. Stockwell then wrote a letter to McDaniel inquiring about the possibility of purchasing Burns, and in early February he received a reply setting the price at $1,300. Stockwell quickly notified Leonard Grimes of the offer to sell Burns, and initially the two clergymen agreed to split the fund-raising responsibilities. Grimes instructed Stockwell to notify McDaniel that his terms were acceptable, and it was agreed that the transfer would be consummated in Baltimore on February 27.

However, it soon became clear that Grimes would bear the entire responsibility of raising the necessary funds, and obtaining the full amount would be more difficult than anticipated. By February 22 he had collected only $676. But on that day, Charles C. Barry, the cashier of City Bank in Boston and secretary of the Pine Street Antislavery Society, advanced Grimes $624 and issued two checks drawn on the Union Bank of Maryland totaling $1,300. With the full purchase price in hand, Grimes set out to meet McDaniel, arriving at Barnum's Hotel in Baltimore at eleven o'clock on the morning of February 27.

In the meantime, with Burns in tow, McDaniel was encountering his own difficulties. Although McDaniel had warned Burns to keep the purpose of their trip secret, on the first leg of the journey—a train ride to Norfolk—it became apparent that others had learned of McDaniel's plan to allow Northerners to purchase Burns's freedom. When the other passengers learned of Burns's presence, they protested loudly, and the conductor declared that if he had been aware of Burns's identity he would not have allowed the slave to board the train. Tensions mounted in Norfolk after McDaniel lodged Burns on a steamer bound for Baltimore and took a brief trip into the city to transact business. McDaniel returned to find Burns surrounded by hostile Norfolk residents who demanded that Burns not be sold to the Bostonians and offered to pay McDaniel $1,500 to purchase Burns themselves. McDaniel, however, refused this offer, declaring that he had already made a bargain and intended to honor it. The crowd then sought to intimidate McDaniel, but he held them at bay with a pistol for an hour and a half. He and Burns were permitted to continue their journey only after McDaniel agreed to return immediately and sell Burns in Norfolk in the event the Bostonians failed to honor their agreement in Baltimore.

McDaniel and Burns met Grimes at the Barnum at approximately 1 PM on February 27. McDaniel demanded payment in cash rather than by check, and the transaction hit a minor snag because the bank required a citizen of Baltimore to certify the identity of the payee, and Grimes did not know anyone in the city. The problem was solved when Grimes endorsed the check to McDaniel, whose identity was then certified by Isaac Barnum, the owner of the hotel. McDaniel then signed the bill of sale after demanding and receiving $25 to cover his expenses.

Fearing that Burns might still be in jeopardy if he remained in a slave state, Grimes determined that he and the now ex-slave should leave Baltimore by train at once. But the two travelers faced one final problem: fearing liability for transporting a fugitive slave north, the railroad would not transport black passengers without a bond of

$1,000. Once again, Barnum came to the rescue by agreeing to sign the bond, and on the night of February 27, Burns slept in Philadelphia, a freeman at last.

For a time, Burns was something of a celebrity in the North. On March 2 and 7 he addressed large crowds in New York and Boston, respectively, briefly describing the circumstances of his capture in Boston and how "a poor fugitive was made a great lion, and escorted out of the free city of Boston . . . amid troops of men armed to the teeth." P. T. Barnum offered Burns $100 per week to tell his story at Barnum's New York museum, but Burns refused, observing disgustedly that "[Barnum] wants to show me like a monkey!" Burns did, however, consent to be exhibited in parts of New England for the benefit of a number of abolitionist societies, and he also became part of a traveling abolitionist show entitled "The Great Moving Mirror of Slavery."

But ultimately, Burns's ambition was to pursue a career as a minister. A Boston woman arranged for Burns to obtain a scholarship to Oberlin College, where he enrolled in the summer of 1855. For the next several years Burns studied at both Oberlin and the Fairmount Theological Seminary in Cincinnati, supporting himself in part by selling copies of an account of his life and rendition written by Charles Emery Stevens. Stevens, a Worcester businessman, had authored the book to advance the antislavery cause in general and the candidacy of Republican John C. Frémont for president in particular. For a short time in 1859 Burns was the minister of an African American church in Indianapolis, but he left that post out of concern that Indiana's law prohibiting the settlement of free African Americans in the state might be enforced against him. Late in 1860 Burns obtained a permanent position leading the black Baptist church in St. Catherines, Ontario, serving in that position until his death from tuberculosis on July 27, 1862. Ironically, shortly before his death, Burns signed a document stating, "Anthony Burns, Ex-Abolitionist: now thinks Lee is the better man."

Thus ended the saga of Anthony Burns. But Burns himself was not the only person whose life was affected by his escape and rendition. Those who were involved in the rescue effort and the rendition itself would also face serious consequences in the mid- and late 1850s.

CHAPTER 9

The Fate of the Rescuers

Apparently unfazed by their inability to gain convictions against the principals in the rescue of Shadrach Minkins, both state and federal officials sought to impose criminal liability on a number of those who had actively participated in the resistance to the rendition of Anthony Burns. The state prosecutions were based on ordinary statutes outlawing murder and "riot." The federal charges did not focus on the claim that the defendants had violated the Fugitive Slave Act per se; rather, they were founded on the theory that those involved in the rescue effort had unlawfully obstructed the execution of legal process by officers of the United States. But despite vigorous efforts by both state and federal officials, none of those who had sought to prevent Burns from being returned were held criminally liable.

State and local officials were the first to act. Martin Stowell and Lewis Hayden each believed that he had fired the fatal shot at Batchelder. However, on June 3 — the day after Burns was removed from Boston — a coroner's jury found that, based on the nature of the mortal wound, an unknown participant in the rescue effort had killed Batchelder with "a long, narrow and sharp instrument." On June 6 and 7 a Boston police court concluded that Stowell and four other persons apprehended during the riot should be charged with murder, and five others should be charged with riot. The court determined that each of the nine should be brought before a municipal grand jury in July.

On June 7 a federal grand jury also began considering the events surrounding the Burns rendition with a charge from Justice Benjamin Robbins Curtis. Not surprisingly, the overall tenor of the charge was less than favorable to the potential defendants. Curtis began with the observation that the murder of Batchelder per se was not a matter with which the federal grand jury should concern itself. But at the same time, the charge defined the concept of "obstruction" broadly enough to potentially cover those who had simply made speeches on the night of the rescue attempt:

> My instruction . . . is that language, addressed to persons who immediately afterwards commit an offence, actually intended by the speaker to incite those addressed to commit it, and adapted thus to incite them, is such a counseling and advising to the crime as the law contemplates, and the person so inciting others is liable to be indicted as a principal.

In addition, although Curtis averred that "it is not my province to comment on events which have recently happened," the language of the charge made his views crystal clear. Noting the difference of opinion between North and South on the issue of fugitive slaves, he continued:

> Who can fail to see that the government would cease to be a government, if it were to yield obedience to those local opinions? While it stands, all its laws must be faithfully executed, or it becomes the mere tool of the strongest faction of the place and the hour. If forcible resistance to one law be permitted practically to repeal it, the power of the mob would inevitably become one of the constituted authorities of the State, to be used against any law or any man obnoxious to the interests and passions of the worst or most excited part of the community; and the peaceful and the weak would be at the mercy of the violent.

Despite this forceful charge, the federal grand jury did not return any indictments. After consulting Attorney General Caleb Cushing, Benjamin Hallett summoned another grand jury to convene in September, and in October he obtained indictments against Higginson, Stowell, Phillips, Parker, and four other men. The indictments averred that the defendants had obstructed federal officials through their participation in the failed rescue effort.

In the interim, a grand jury had been impaneled in July in municipal court in Boston to consider a wide variety of issues, including the charges leveled by the police court. The presiding judge was Ebenezer R. Hoar of the Massachusetts Court of Common Pleas. Like the Curtises, Hoar's family was prominent in the Massachusetts Whig Party. However, Hoar was far more committed to the antislavery cause; he was an erstwhile Conscience Whig and had been a leader in organizing the Free-Soil Party in Massachusetts. Hoar's charge to the grand jury reflected a complex interaction between this commitment and an equally strong attachment to the concept of the rule of law.

Hoar made no secret of his distaste for both the Fugitive Slave Act and Shaw's opinion in *Sims* upholding the constitutionality of the statute. He declared that the statute "seems to me to evince a more deliberate and settled disregard of all the principles of constitutional liberty than any other enactment which has ever come under my notice." Further, he asserted that Shaw's opinion "is placed on the ground of authority, rather than of right," and that "the authorities upon which that decision rests have failed to satisfy my understanding."

In addition, Hoar sharply criticized the use of the militia to transfer Burns from the courthouse to the ship, contending that "there is no law in this Commonwealth by which any district or part of a city or town, can be put in possession of a military force in time of peace, with power to obstruct the ordinary and reasonable use of the public ways, and to prevent peaceable citizens from transacting their lawful business — merely on account of an anticipated riot." Further, he stated, "the fact that a riot has previously taken place, unless it be continuous and existing, will not alter [this] rule of law." Hoar explicitly called on the grand jury to hold members of the military escort itself to account "if it shall be made to appear to you that any assault has been committed, or violence done, or forcible obstruction of lawful business occasioned" without proper justification.

Yet at the same time, Hoar clearly instructed the grand jury to hold the rescuers themselves legally responsible for any violations of existing law. Despite his expressed distaste for the Fugitive Slave Act and Shaw's opinion in *Sims*, Hoar declared that "whatever opinions we may individually maintain as to the correctness of [the decision in *Sims*] no citizen of the Commonwealth has a legal right to disregard the decision of the Supreme Court. . . . It is the duty of every inferior tribunal to regard what they have decided henceforth as law, and it is the duty of all those concerned in the administration of justice . . . so to regard it. Gentlemen, any other rule, any other conclusion, could lead to nothing but anarchy." Turning to the claim that "there are laws which it is the duty of citizens to disobey or resist," Hoar asserted, "it is not a question of private conscience which determines our duties in [these] premises. A man whose private conscience leads him to disobey a law recognized by the community, must take the consequences of that disobedience." Based on this charge, the grand jury refused to indict the eight defendants for murder, but it did indict them for riot. However, the defendants were never tried on these charges, apparently because the court docket was clogged with liquor cases, which, by statute, were given priority over all other criminal cases.

By contrast, at least initially, the federal authorities were more aggressive in pursuing the charges against those involved in the assault on the courthouse. In late October Hallett dispatched Asa Butman to Worcester to gather evidence and subpoena witnesses for the upcoming trial. A member of the Boston Vigilance Committee alerted his counterparts in Worcester, and on October 29 Butman's hotel was surrounded by members of the Worcester committee with the avowed purpose of monitoring his movements. Butman produced a pistol and stated that he was ready to use it, whereupon he was promptly arrested by the local authorities on a charge of carrying a concealed weapon.

The following day Butman was taken before the local police court for arraignment, where his case was postponed for two weeks. The courtroom was surrounded by an angry crowd, and it was decided that Butman should be returned to Boston. But the crowd did not disperse, even after being ordered to do so by the mayor. Instead, it grew to over 1,000 strong, with a number of people loudly threatening Butman with bodily harm.

At this point, ironically, Butman was saved by a representative of the very forces he had infuriated by his own conduct during the rendition of Anthony Burns. George Hoar, the brother of Ebenezer, reminded the crowd that his father, Samuel, had been subjected to similar treatment during his 1844 mission to South Carolina to challenge the Negro Seamen's Act, but that he had been allowed to depart unharmed. Hoar, together with Martin Stowell and Thomas Higginson, then joined five policemen to escort Butman to the local train station.

Despite being pelted with stones and rotten eggs, Butman arrived at the station without suffering serious injuries. However, he missed the train and was forced to return to Boston in an enclosed wagon, which suffered broken windows as the rock throwing continued. After arriving in Boston, Butman swore that he would never return to Worcester.

Despite this setback, Hallett was determined to move forward with the trial. The defendants' attitudes toward the proceedings differed widely. Whereas Stowell was worried that he might be convicted, Phillips and Parker viewed the impending trial as another opportunity to advance the abolitionist cause. Fellow Massachusetts abolitionist Samuel May Jr. aptly summarized their attitude when he wrote privately that Phillips and Parker "will doubtless have a magnificent triumph over their prosecutors" and "the *cause* will certainly triumph, even if despotism should succeed in fining and imprisoning *them*."

The trial before Judge Sprague and Justice Curtis was originally scheduled to begin on March 5, 1855, but the arraignment of the eight defendants was postponed until April 3 to accommodate Curtis's schedule on the Supreme Court. The government had attempted to secure the services of Rufus Choate, an eminent conservative Whig lawyer, to join Hallett in representing the government, but Choate refused and urged Hallett to drop the charges. Instead, Hallett was assisted by Elias Merwin, who had been Curtis's law partner. The defendants were represented by a team of five antislavery lawyers: John A. Andrew, William L. Burt, Henry Durant, Charles M. Ellis, and John P. Hale.

When the court convened on April 3, the defendants pleaded not guilty and then, with the exception of Parker, immediately walked out of the courtroom in protest against what they described as "Curtisdom." Hale moved to quash the indictments, and the defense attorneys raised six different procedural points in support of Hale's motion. After hearing arguments on these points, Curtis found on April 12, in *United States v. Stowell*, that the indictments were fatally defective. But in reaching this conclusion, Curtis did not rely on any of the contentions raised by the defense lawyers. According to Curtis, the difficulty was that, for the defendants to have committed a criminal offense, they must have interfered with a legal process that had been issued by an officer with legitimate authority to issue such process. Although the commissioners appointed to enforce the Fugitive Slave Act possessed such authority, the indictment identified Edward Loring only as "a commissioner of the circuit court," without specifying his precise duties. Citing the principle that "an indictment must contain every averment necessary to show that an offense has been committed," Curtis concluded that because *some* commissioners lacked the requisite authority, the indictment was fatally flawed.

Curtis needed to go no further to resolve the criminal charges before him. Nonetheless, he chose to explicitly address two of the objections raised by the defense attorneys, both of which involved the manner in which members of the grand jury had been selected. Curtis first discussed in detail and rejected the claim that the list from which the grand jurors had been selected improperly excluded potential jurors from the "remote, interior towns" of Massachusetts. He then briefly turned to the claim that the grand jury had been improperly constituted because Marshal Freeman, who was in charge of selecting the jurors, was not an "indifferent" person as required by statute—in essence, that because Freeman might have been biased, he could have stacked the grand jury with members who were unsympathetic to the defendants' alleged conduct.

This contention was particularly explosive in light of the fact that Freeman had chosen William Greenough, Curtis's brother-in-law and presumably a person hostile to the defendants, as a member of the grand jury that had handed down the indictments. Indeed, Curtis himself averred that "if it had been alleged that the marshal, or any other person concerned in returning the grand jury, had been guilty of any unfair or improper conduct in forming the panel, we should have deemed it our duty carefully and promptly to investigate the charge." But, Curtis observed, no such specific charge had been made. Instead, the defense lawyers had alleged only that, in the abstract, by virtue of his position, the marshal was not legally qualified to assemble the grand jury. Characterizing this question as "attended with difficulty," Curtis chose to leave it unresolved because it was not critical to the disposition of the case before him.

In *Stowell*, Curtis acknowledged that his decision did not foreclose Hallett from obtaining revised indictments that specified the source of Loring's power to issue the warrants. However, it soon became clear that this possibility was more theoretical than real. When Hallett petitioned to reconvene the same grand jury that had handed down the defective indictments, the petition was denied on the ground that

Freeman, who had selected the members of that body, had not been an "indifferent person" as required by statute. Subsequently, in private conversations, Curtis and Sprague dissuaded Hallett from further efforts to reindict the defendants, observing that the original warrant for Burns's arrest was defective because it failed to adequately describe the source of Loring's authority to issue the warrant, and thus Phillips, Parker, and their compatriots could not be convicted for resisting a legal process.

In sharp contrast to Hallett's reaction, Curtis's decision to quash the indictment was greeted by "considerable applause" in the courtroom, and the *Liberator* opined, "thus endeth a grand legal farce . . . which has been admirably played for all purposes of agitation and excitement, but which has been simply ridiculous from beginning to end." The more conservative *Boston Daily Advertiser* praised the "quiet conclusion" of the criminal action, noting that "many an anxious eye" had seen "threatening clouds" overhanging the trial. Similarly, die-hard conservative Whig Edward Everett observed that, given the climate of opinion, there was almost no possibility of a conviction in any event and continued:

> The trial would only have afforded the defendants a new chance to insult the Court and defy the law. Had they been, contrary to all probability, convicted, this would have been to them the greatest of triumphs. It would have made them martyrs; their fines would have been paid by [others]; and if they had been sent to prison, they would have spoken with far greater effect from gaol than from the platform or the pulpit.

Parker was less satisfied with the quick dismissal. He had been planning to use the trial as a platform from which to launch public attacks against Bostonians who continued to advocate compromise with the South and had been busily preparing an elaborate presentation of his position. Notwithstanding the dismissal of the charges against him, he published and distributed *The Trial of Theodore Parker, for the "Misdemeanor" of a Speech at Faneuil Hall*, an extraordinary combination of legal argument and political polemic. In the tract, Parker attacked the charges against him as infringements on freedom of speech and freedom of religion. He also launched a detailed assault on the constitutionality of the Fugitive Slave Act, as well as in-depth defenses of the concept of jury nullification and appeals to the concept of "Higher Law."

In addition, Parker took the opportunity to vigorously press his critique of the influence of the slave power, as well as those whom he characterized as collaborators with the pro-slavery forces. Although he harshly criticized the actions of both Daniel Webster and Peleg Sprague, much of Parker's attack was aimed explicitly at the Curtis family. Parker provided a detailed list of cases in which the Curtises had supported the institution of slavery. He cited Benjamin R. Curtis in particular, noting that he "was apparently destitute of any high moral instincts" and claiming that "no lawyer in New England [has] laid down such Southern 'principles' for foundation of law [and none has] rendered such service to the slave power."

Of course, as a sitting justice of the U.S. Supreme Court, Curtis was largely immune from the practical consequences of his failure to fully embrace the antislavery viewpoint. In contrast, as a member of the Curtis family, Edward Loring was far more vulnerable. And indeed, Loring's punishment for his actions in the Burns case became an important objective of much of the Massachusetts antislavery establishment.

CHAPTER 10

Loring under Attack

Loring was vilified in much of Massachusetts from the moment he ordered Anthony Burns returned to Virginia. Soon after Loring rendered his judgment, Richard Henry Dana published a direct challenge to the legal reasoning underlying the rendition decision in the *Boston Atlas*. "The Decision Which Judge Loring Might Have Given" recapitulated a number of the arguments made by Dana and Charles Ellis in their defense of Burns. Dana argued that even though section 10 of the Fugitive Slave Act made the record of the Virginia court conclusive on the issues of possession and escape, the conclusive presumption could not be invoked in the face of Brent's testimony, which, in Dana's view, indicated that only Millspaugh, not Suttle, had the lawful authority to obtain a certificate under the statute. Moreover, on the issue of identity, Dana contended that if Burns's statement to Suttle were admissible, the court would also have to accept Burns's account of how he came to be in Boston, which rebutted any inference that he was an escapee.

Not surprisingly, many residents of Massachusetts went well beyond simple criticism of Loring's legal reasoning. Loring was burned in effigy numerous times, and many argued that more extreme measures were appropriate. For example, one particularly strident critic declared, "he should be driven from city to city, a pilgrim and a stranger. Let him be pointed out to the little children, as he passes through the streets, as the KIDNAPPER of men, the manufacturer of widows and orphans." A correspondent of the *Boston Commonwealth* expressed similar sentiments in slightly less inflammatory language, asserting that Loring "ought to be held infamous by the people of Boston and Massachusetts. . . . Let him be a marked man forever." The weight of public opinion took its toll on Loring; after visiting Loring in September 1854, Samuel Gridley Howe reported that "he looked much changed [and] seemed to me to have lost all interest in life."

Not content with simple expressions of outrage, the antislavery forces sought to punish Loring in more tangible ways by stripping him of his professional positions. The first issue that came to a head was a struggle over Loring's reappointment to his position at Harvard Law School. Like Massachusetts society more generally, the Harvard community was divided over Loring's conduct of the rendition proceedings—a division that was only deepened by the presence of a significant contingent of Southern students at the law school, a number of whom had volunteered to act as bodyguards for Suttle during his sojourn in Boston. Indeed, Loring's effort to teach his class on the Friday after the rendition hearing commenced had created considerable controversy: he had been hissed at by antislavery students, while their Southern classmates had greeted Loring with "thunders of welcome and shouts of approval." As already noted, John G. Palfrey, a committed Free-Soiler and member of the Harvard Board of Overseers, had urged Loring to either abandon his duties as a fugitive slave commissioner or resign his post at the law school.

Harvard's complex governing structure added to Loring's difficulties. In addition to requiring the recommendation of other members of the law school faculty, his reappointment needed to be endorsed by two separate bodies. The seven-person Harvard Corporation was a generally conservative group composed entirely of members of the Boston elite, such as Lemuel Shaw. In contrast, the much larger Board of Overseers included many government officials, and its membership was drawn from across Massachusetts, including several members who were strongly committed to the antislavery movement. Against this background, the professors at the law school strongly urged Loring's reappointment, describing him as a "useful and acceptable man," and on August 26, 1854, the Fellows of the Harvard Corporation concurred, recommending that the Board of Overseers reappoint Loring at its upcoming meeting in February 1855.

As the date of this meeting approached, partisans on both sides of the issue intensified their campaigns. The *National Anti-Slavery Standard* declared that Loring's reappointment would "give to the infamous fugitive slave law and to its mercenary executors, the indorsement of Massachusetts through her highest seminary of learning," and the *New York Tribune* expressed similar sentiments. Conversely, the Curtis family and their allies made strenuous efforts to secure Loring's reappointment. George Ticknor Curtis penned an anonymous pamphlet, noting that by bringing students from all sections of the country together, the law school "has been a very powerful instrument *in removing and softening sectional prejudices.*" If Loring were denied reappointment under these circumstances, he suggested, Southern families would be reluctant to send their children to Harvard. This argument proved to be of no avail; on February 15, by a vote of 20–10, the Board of Overseers rejected the recommendation of the Harvard Corporation and refused to reappoint Loring.

Understandably, the decision of the overseers gave great satisfaction to the antislavery forces. The *New York Independent* rejoiced that "kidnapping has been rebuked in conservative Harvard," and the Chicago correspondent of the *Salem Observer* declared, "nothing can exceed the gratification that the people here feel for the manly action of the overseers of Harvard College in the rejection of . . . Loring." The *New York Tribune* was even more expansive in its praise: "We rejoice at such a declaration of public sentiment. It does not come a day too soon, and we trust that it will have its due influence in other States. The slave catcher and the Slave Commissioner must be made to feel that they lie under the ban of general loathing, something like that which, in the Middle Ages, rested on the professional hangman and torturer."

However, support for the overseers' action was far from uniform. For example, the *Boston Daily Advertiser* declared, "the appointment was eminently a fit and excellent one," and "the shame of this proceeding falls on the twenty Overseers [who voted against Loring]." Not surprisingly, the Southerners who constituted a substantial part of the student body were particularly incensed. After a series of tumultuous meetings of the law school's student organization, Southern students succeeded in pushing through a resolution expressing regret at Loring's departure and condemning what it described as the "tyrannical and ungenerous" conduct of the overseers. Similarly, in a letter to the *Savannah Daily Morning News*, the parent of a student from the South attributed the action of the Board of Overseers to a spirit of "abolitionism and fanaticism" and suggested that the refusal to reappoint Loring should lead other slave owners to reconsider the wisdom of sending their children to Harvard.

The decision of the Board of Overseers was made in the midst of a concerted effort to remove Loring from his position as a probate judge. This effort evolved against the backdrop of an extraordinary upheaval in the structure of Massachusetts politics. With antislavery sentiment widespread in Massachusetts and the national Democratic Party irrevocably associated with the Kansas-Nebraska Act, Henry Wilson and many other Free-Soilers advanced the idea of forming a fusion antislavery party with Massachusetts Whigs. But, resentful of the fact that the Free-Soilers had joined with the Democrats in an anti-Whig coalition in the early 1850s, even Whigs with strong antislavery sentiments—increasingly dominant within their own party—were unwilling to join with their erstwhile enemies. Instead, the Whigs sought to establish themselves as the primary vehicle for antislavery action in the state. In June the party's central committee issued a statement strongly condemning the Free-Soilers for their recent participation in a governing coalition with the Democrats, and the Whig state convention adopted a platform calling for repeal of the Kansas-Nebraska Act and either repeal of the Fugitive Slave Act or, at the very least, a dramatic alteration of the statute to provide much greater procedural protections for alleged escapees. The convention then chose Emory Washburn to be its standard-bearer in the gubernatorial contest.

Undaunted, Henry Wilson led a group of Free-Soilers in calling for a fusion convention that met in Worcester on September 6. Although dominated by Free-Soilers, the convention adopted the name "Republican" and an uncompromisingly antislavery platform. The rechristened party then chose Wilson as its candidate for governor. However, in the elections of 1854, both the Whigs and the Republicans were eclipsed by an entirely new organization—the Know-Nothing Party.

The Know-Nothing Party was not open to the general public. Rather, party membership was limited to those who joined a network of lodges whose proceedings were shrouded in secrecy and whose members were instructed to claim that they "knew nothing" if asked about the lodges. The basic ideology of the party did not have its origins in the dispute over slavery. Rather, in theory, party members were united by a commitment to the principles of nativism, with a particular emphasis on hostility to the Irish Catholics who had immigrated to Massachusetts in droves in the late 1840s and early 1850s.

However, with the state Democratic Party discredited over slavery and the Whigs failing to deliver on their promise to reform state government, the Know-Nothing Party and the lodges themselves became magnets for those who were dissatisfied with the existing structure of Massachusetts politics, including many who had previously rejected nativism. Many of the converts were Free-Soilers who hoped to use the Know-Nothing movement as a vehicle to advance the antislavery agenda.

The prominence of Irish American militiamen in the defense of the courthouse during the Burns rendition hearings and the perceived support of Catholics for the national Democratic Party may have encouraged some antislavery activists to join hands with the nativists. For example, Theodore Parker asserted that "the Catholic clergy are on the side of slavery," and in June 1854 the *Boston Commonwealth* complained that "the Catholic press upholds the slave power and seeks to annihilate those who resist its atrocious doctrines and doings. These two malign powers have a natural affinity for each other."

Although many of the Know-Nothings were refugees from the Free-Soil Party, Henry J. Gardner, who became the Know-Nothing candidate for governor, was cut from a different cloth. Gardner was an obscure former state legislator who, in the early 1850s, had been an ardent supporter of Daniel Webster. As a member of the Boston Common Council, Gardner had stood alone in openly supporting Millard Fillmore's proclamation condemning the rescuers of Shadrach Minkins, and he had purportedly volunteered to assist in the rendition of Thomas Sims. But in 1854 Gardner suddenly embraced the antislavery cause, publicly condemning both the Kansas-Nebraska Act and the Fugitive Slave Act.

Gardner owed his nomination largely to the support of Henry Wilson and his allies. Even before he obtained the Republican nomination for governor, Wilson had joined a Know-Nothing lodge. He threw his support behind Gardner in exchange for a promise of Know-Nothing support in Wilson's bid to fill the unexpired U.S. Senate term of conservative Whig Edward Everett, who had resigned amid public outcry at his failure to appear to vote against the Kansas-Nebraska Act because of illness. After Gardner received the Know-

Nothing nomination on October 18, Wilson completed his part of the bargain by formally withdrawing from the gubernatorial contest, too late for the Republicans to substitute a different candidate.

In the November election the Know-Nothing Party won a stunning victory. Gardner received 62 percent of the vote for governor, easily defeating Washburn and two other candidates. Even more amazingly, the Know-Nothings carried all eleven congressional districts and 411 of 419 seats in the state legislature. The Know-Nothing victory was also a victory for the antislavery forces: seven of the eleven newly elected congressmen were former Free-Soilers, and almost a third of the members of the lower house of the state legislature voted to appoint Theodore Parker as their chaplain. But not all Massachusetts Know-Nothings were so strongly committed to the antislavery movement. Thus, the effort to remove Loring from his probate judgeship in 1855 provoked internecine warfare in the newly dominant party.

Those who sought to strip Loring of his commission did not initiate impeachment proceedings under chapter I, section 3, article VI, of the state constitution. Instead, they invoked chapter III, article I, which stated that judges should hold their offices during "good behavior" but also provided that "the governor, with consent of the council, may remove [judges] upon the address of both houses of the legislature." The basic concept of removal by address — apparently borrowed from the English parliamentary system — was by no means unique to the Massachusetts constitution, but the Massachusetts provision was unusual in that it did not require a supermajority of the legislature for removal.

Although the debates surrounding the inclusion of this provision in the 1780 constitution were not recorded, exercise of the removal power was, by its terms, committed entirely to the discretion of the legislature and the governor. Still, the idea that a judge could be removed in this manner might be viewed as being in some tension with the principle that judges should have life tenure, subject only to the requirement of "good behavior" — a concept plainly designed to free the judiciary from the influence of the political branches.

In any event, prior to 1855, the removal provision had been invoked against only three sitting judges. The removal of Justice Theophilius Bradbury of the Supreme Judicial Court was accomplished without dissent. Bradbury had suffered a debilitating stroke the previous year from which he was unlikely to recover. Given that impeachment was plainly inappropriate, removal by address was the only device available to rid the court of a justice who had become unable to perform his duties through no fault of his own. Thus, all apparently agreed that Bradbury's situation presented the paradigm case for removal.

Justices Paul Dudley Sargent and William Vinall of the Court of Common Pleas presented more controversial cases. Both were removed after being convicted in criminal court of using their offices for "willful and corrupt extortion." John Quincy Adams (then a state senator) dissented, contending that impeachment was the only appropriate remedy in such cases. Adams argued that the state legislature should not be bound by the findings of a criminal jury and that Sargent and Vinall should have been given an opportunity to defend themselves against the charges in an impeachment trial.

Against this background, a concerted effort was made to change the removal provision during the Massachusetts Constitutional Convention of 1820. Declaring that "this provision has a tendency materially to impair the independence of the judges, and to destroy the efficacy of the clause which declares they shall hold their offices during good behavior," a committee composed of Joseph Story, Lemuel Shaw, and twelve other luminaries of the state bar proposed to amend the constitution to require a two-thirds majority from each house to effectuate removal. On the convention floor, Daniel Webster raised a different concern, arguing that the removal provision should be amended to require that any judge who was the subject of removal proceedings be given notice of the accusation against him and an opportunity to be heard in his defense. In contrast, Levi Lincoln, who would later become both a justice on the Supreme Judicial Court and governor of Massachusetts, declared himself "entirely satisfied with the constitution as it is," and Henry H. Child asserted that "it [would be] in violation of an important principle of the government [if] the majority of the Legislature, together with the Governor, should not have the power of removal from office."

Ultimately, Webster's proposal was included in the document approved by the convention and was submitted for ratification by the people as part of an amendment that also would have eliminated the authority of the state legislature and the governor to obtain the

Supreme Judicial Court's opinion on important issues of law. However, the proposed amendment was defeated in the referendum. Thus, the unaltered language from the 1780 constitution became the basis of the effort to remove Loring.

Within a week of the decision in the Burns case, the Massachusetts Anti-Slavery Society began to circulate petitions demanding Loring's removal from office. Antislavery women distributed analogous petitions. Ultimately, the state legislature received well over 100 such petitions favoring removal, with a total of more than 10,000 signatures.

Invited by the legislature to respond to these petitions, Loring declined to appear in person. Instead, on February 9, 1855, he sent a written response. After observing that he held his position as a commissioner under the authority of the Fugitive Slave Act of 1850 and that the constitutionality of this statute had been upheld by the Supreme Judicial Court of Massachusetts, Loring argued that because the act provided that commissioners were "*required* to exercise all the powers and duties conferred by [the statute]," he could not have legally refused to exercise jurisdiction over Suttle's application for the rendition of Burns. Thus, Loring contended, in presiding over the rendition proceeding, he was simply honoring his oath of office. Moreover, he observed that no official of the Massachusetts state government had ever suggested to him that service as a commissioner in proceedings under the Fugitive Slave Act was in any way incompatible with his duties as a probate judge. Under these circumstances, Loring contended that to remove him from office would be "an abuse of power for which the legislative history of Massachusetts furnishes no precedent." He reiterated this point on February 19, asserting that "conformity to the Constitution and laws of the United States is not a reason for withdrawing from a judicial officer that security which the Constitution of Massachusetts assures him during 'good behavior.'"

The Curtis family also made a strong effort to rally support for Loring. One hundred seventy-four Boston lawyers joined a petition endorsing Loring's argument, and remonstrances against removal were signed by almost 1,000 other Bostonians and more than 300 other citizens of Massachusetts. Similarly, the *Daily Advertiser* proclaimed that the reasoning of Loring's response was "irrefutable" and averred that his removal would be "an outrageous assault on the independence of the judiciary." Nonetheless, as the state legislature began its consideration of Loring's future, public sentiment seemed to be in favor of stripping him of his judicial post.

Formal hearings opened on February 20, 1855, before the Committee on Federal Relations of the state house of representatives. Recognizing the tremendous public interest in the proceedings, the committee convened in the great hall of the statehouse rather than its usual smaller venue. But even the larger facility could not accommodate all those who wished to attend the hearings. The great hall was filled to capacity, and hundreds of other interested citizens filled the streets outside.

The first day was given over to attacks on Loring from Seth Webb, Charles Ellis, and Wendell Phillips. Their presentations were laced with polemical attacks that expressed the antislavery community's outrage at Loring's actions in the Burns case. Thus, Phillips declared, "to consent actively to aid in hunting slaves here and now, shows a hardness of heart, a merciless spirit, a moral blindness, an utter spiritual death, that totally unfit a man for the judicial office." Webb asserted that "it is not fit that the man on whom rests the spotless ermine of the Massachusetts judiciary should bow down to false gods, and go into the house of the strange Southern women." Ellis stated that "Massachusetts . . . cannot be true to her conscience and allow [Loring] to remain in office."

Phillips was primarily responsible for translating this outrage into a detailed legal justification for removing Loring. Phillips's first task was to formulate a general standard for determining when the removal provision should be invoked. The battle over the proper interpretation of the removal provision was part of a larger dispute over the proper role of judges in the system of government generally. Whigs typically emphasized the need to preserve judicial independence and objectivity through devices such as life tenure. Democrats, by contrast, generally emphasized the need to protect against judicial tyranny, arguing that judges should be elected for limited terms and that juries should be given the power to make independent judgments on issues of law as well as fact.

In the Loring case itself, the provisions of the Massachusetts Personal Liberty Law of 1843 complicated the problem. That statute forbade state officials from aiding specifically in the enforcement of the

Fugitive Slave Act of 1793. The difficulty was that Loring held the office of federal commissioner not under that statute but under the authority of the Fugitive Slave Act of 1850. Given that the antislavery forces in the Massachusetts legislature had tried and failed to update the personal liberty law in 1851, the question was whether the 1843 statute had any bearing on the propriety of Loring's decision to preside over the Burns rendition proceeding.

Against this background, Phillips first distinguished sharply between the removal provision and the impeachment provision. He conceded that, to warrant impeachment, a judge must have committed some misconduct in his official capacity. In contrast, drawing extensively on the legislative history of the removal provision, he contended that a judge could "be removed . . . for any cause which the Legislature, in its discretion, thinks a fitting cause for his removal." Phillips admitted that "this is a grave power, and one to be used only on important occasions. We are bound to show you, not light and trifling reasons for the removal of Judge Loring, but such grave and serious reasons, such weighty cause, as will justify your interference, and make the use of your authority to strengthen rather than weaken the proper independence of the bench."

Phillips then listed a number of reasons that he believed were sufficient to justify Loring's removal. He first asserted that simply by participating in the rendition process, Loring had "acted in defiance of the solemn convictions and settled purposes of Massachusetts." Despite the fact that, by its terms, the prohibition in the Personal Liberty Law of 1843 applied only to the Fugitive Slave Act of 1793, Phillips argued that aiding in the enforcement of the Fugitive Slave Act of 1850 was no less offensive to the expressed policy of the state. He noted that in *Sims*, Chief Justice Shaw had relied on the similarities between the two statutes in upholding the 1850 law, and that in September 1850 the state legislature had passed a resolution condemning the new statute because it did not provide for jury trials and proclaiming that "the people of Massachusetts . . . expect that all their officers and representatives will adhere to [this view] on all occasions, and under all circumstances." Later, returning to the same theme, Phillips declared, "when a Judge violates the well-known, mature, religious conviction of the State on a grave and vital question of practical morality, having had full warning, such violation shall be held sufficient cause for his removal."

Phillips further claimed that, even if Loring's decision to participate in the rendition proceeding was unobjectionable on its own terms, the manner in which the proceeding had been conducted justified Loring's removal from office. In addition to reprising Dana's criticisms of Loring's analysis of the facts and the law, Phillips lodged a number of complaints against Loring's conduct of the proceeding. The most serious charge was that Loring had prejudged the case before hearing the evidence. In support of this claim, Phillips cited two incidents. First, Phillips reported that when granting his request to visit Burns, Loring had told Phillips, "this case is so clear, that I do not think you will be justified in placing any obstacles in the way of this man's going back, as he probably will." Second, Phillips asserted that by writing the bill of sale for the abortive transaction that would have conveyed Burns to Leonard Grimes on May 27, Loring had in essence conceded Suttle's title to Burns. Phillips also raised a number of other objections to Loring's treatment of the case, including the rumor that Loring had given Suttle and the city authorities advance notice of his decision.

But the core of Phillips's argument remained that Massachusetts should not tolerate a judge who was actively involved in enforcement of the Fugitive Slave Act. Phillips was careful to note that the legislature was not being asked to deny citizens the right to act as commissioners under the statute, but simply to conclude that those who participated in the rendition process should not simultaneously be allowed to continue as state judges. He conceded that "it is, unfortunately, [Loring's] right as a citizen of the United States, to take part in slave hunts." But Phillips also contended that "the Commonwealth has, also . . . the right to say that her Judges shall be decent men at least. Make your choice!"

In addition to excoriating Loring's behavior in the Burns case, Phillips addressed the claim that removal of the probate judge would undermine the independence of the judiciary. Phillips contended that, by removing Loring, "we are cutting off a corrupt member and securing for the rest the only source of strength, the confidence of the Commonwealth. The Bench is not weakened when we remove a bad Judge, but when we retain him. . . . If any man here loves the Judiciary, and wishes to secure its independence and its influence with the people, let him aid us to cut off the offending member." He also asserted that it would be "far better . . . to have, for Judges, dependent honest men, than independent slave catchers."

The February 20 hearing ended, and the committee scheduled another meeting for February 28, when the opponents of removal were expected to present their case. However, the defense of Loring did not materialize at that time. The reluctance of many in the political establishment to appear on Loring's behalf was a by-product of a variety of factors. First, distaste for Loring's ruling in the Burns case extended well beyond the radical antislavery community represented by men such as Phillips, Webb, and Ellis. For example, the more moderate Samuel Bowles, editor of the *Springfield Republican*, asserted that the removal of Loring would demonstrate that Massachusetts "will neither obey nor resist the Fugitive Slave law." Second, some who otherwise might have rallied to defend the concept of an independent judiciary characterized Loring's situation as a special case without precedential significance. Thus, Josiah Quincy, former mayor of Boston and president of Harvard University, contended that Loring's removal would not be taken as a strong precedent in the future because "an irresponsible hand" — that is, the Know-Nothing–dominated legislature — would have "struck the blow," and Bowles expressed the fear that if Loring were not removed, "the advocates of an elective judiciary for a short term will double instanter in Massachusetts, and our judiciary will be placed where every passing popular breeze can reach them."

Loring's close association with the Curtis family also worked to his disadvantage. Quincy asserted that "he wished to [see] Loring punished, and his set, the clique of the Curtises put down." Antislavery lawyer Franklin Dexter claimed that he would have come to Loring's aid "were it not for [Dexter's] extreme dislike [for] the Curtis faction." Conversely, the Curtises and their close associates chose not to present arguments before the committee either because they believed that highlighting their association with Loring would hurt his cause or because they simply wanted to avoid subjecting themselves to questioning from such a hostile group of legislators.

Thus, when the committee reconvened on February 28 — the day after Grimes purchased Burns's freedom in Baltimore — the proceedings were once again dominated by antislavery activists. Phillips gave additional testimony, and statements were made by Theodore Parker,

Robert Morris, Amasa Walker, and Richard Hildreth. Morris — an abolitionist lawyer who had been prosecuted in the wake of the Shadrach Minkins rescue — contended that Loring had "hurried the [Burns] case as much as circumstances would permit . . . more than any other slave commissioner would have done." Walker stated that "it was time for Massachusetts to do something to assert her rights and sovereignty as a state" by removing Loring.

Hildreth was the featured speaker for the pro-removal forces. Rejecting the claim that removal would inappropriately threaten judicial independence, Hildreth declared that "judges are the agents and substitutes for the people [who have the right] to change our agents and return them to private life." Implicitly decrying the power of the Curtises and their associates, he asserted that "independence of the judiciary was not in danger from public sentiment, but from influences apart from the people, which sought to control public opinion and action." Hildreth suggested darkly that the *Sims* decision had been a product of a wish to advance Webster's presidential ambitions and claimed that Loring "desires to be a martyr for the fugitive slave act, because such martyrdom may lead to some well paid federal office." In addition, Hildreth argued that "Judge Loring's personal interest in his office is a trifling matter," that the issue of removal was a question of "public interest," and that "the slaveholders had an interest, and it was very proper that they should be heard."

Against this background, John W. Gitchell purported to speak in support of Loring. Gitchell represented himself as a plantation owner and slaveholder in Jacksonville, Alabama, who had migrated from Pennsylvania. He stated that when stopping over in Boston on his way home from a business trip, he had heard of the committee's proceedings and wished to speak on behalf of the South. Gitchell's testimony on February 28 was actually his second appearance before the Committee on Federal Relations. On February 13 he had participated in hearings on a proposal to adopt a new personal liberty law. In both cases, Gitchell's presentations, which were described as "crude, coarse and illiterate," were so ineffective as to be counterproductive. Indeed, some suspected that he had actually been solicited by the antislavery forces to epitomize the ignorant Southern planter whom they characterized as forming the backbone of the "slave power" that threatened the free-labor values of the North.

Despite the fact that none of them spoke at the February 28 hearing, some prominent members of the Massachusetts political establishment voiced public opposition to Loring's removal. The opponents of removal often denounced Loring's views but focused on the need to preserve judicial independence. For example, prominent Free-Soiler Samuel Sewall wrote that "nothing could be more impolitic than to remove Judge Loring, for his obnoxious opinions, in the way proposed. . . . If this principle be admitted, every Legislature in its turn would ostracize all political opponents within its reach, till the power of legislative removal would become [an] odious and corrupting . . . engine of party despotism." Ironically, however, when the committee reconvened on March 5, it was Richard Henry Dana who became the public face of the anti-removal forces.

The March 5 hearing began with testimony from Hamilton Willis, who described Loring's role in the failed effort to purchase Burns's freedom on May 27. Willis's testimony was followed by a fiery speech from Theodore Parker in support of the removal effort. Contending that the removal power was "limited only by a condition that the act of removal shall be in conformity with the law of God," Parker declared that "the cause of complaint against [Loring] as a judge is that he *stole a man*" and stated, "we ask Loring's removal because we have a kidnapper as a Judge of Probate, one who kidnaps on principle." He further asserted that "if there were no God in heaven, no golden rule, no conscience in men, then the course of Mr. Loring might be justified; but while they exist, they cannot be justified."

Dana followed Parker and spoke for nearly four hours. He began by observing that if only Loring's personal fate were at issue, and if Dana believed that the probate judge could be removed "justly and safely [and] consistent[ly] with the dignity of Massachusetts," Dana himself might well have supported the removal to demonstrate that the state was "earnest" in its opposition to the Fugitive Slave Act. But Dana argued that what was at stake was not simply the fate of Loring in isolation but rather the principle of judicial independence more generally, averring, "we all have a deep stake in the tenure of the judicial office, and the immunity of judges in all but the clearest and most unequivocal cases."

In making this argument, Dana focused on the role of the judiciary in constitutional interpretation. He contended that if removal by address were a common practice, legislatures could easily circumvent constitutional constraints on their power, arguing, "you have only to remove from office by address, the judges who differ from you, and you make yourselves the supreme judicature, and the final interpreters of the Constitution." He also observed that the removal power had been used previously in only two cases, one of which was a confessed case of senility. Finally, like Sewall, Dana warned that the theory of the removal power being deployed against Loring could easily be turned against other judges in the future, asserting, "if you remove Judge Loring because he executed the Fugitive Slave Law, other judges . . . may be removed because they do not." He then asked, "would you desire each successive Legislature . . . revising the list of the judges of the land, and trying each by its tests of 'piety,' 'temperance,' 'moderation,' 'frugality,' and 'fidelity to the fundamental principles of the Constitution.' Would not the evils of such a censorship be likely to be greater than its advantages?"

Noting that arch-radical Charles Sumner had volunteered to act as a commissioner under the Fugitive Slave Act, Dana scoffed at the notion that, taken alone, Loring's decision to preside over the rendition proceeding justified his removal. Instead, Dana focused his attention on the claim that, "in the conduct of the [Burns] case, [Loring] exhibited traits of character which show him unfit for the office of Judge, and rendered him so justly odious that the public interests require his removal." The picture he painted of Loring's conduct of the rendition hearing differed markedly from Phillips's portrayal. Dana read a contemporaneous entry from his own journal that observed, "the conduct of Judge Loring has been considerate and humane. If a man is willing to execute the law, and be an instrument of sending back a man into slavery under such a law, he could not act better in his office than Judge Loring."

Dana focused particular attention on the events that took place immediately after he entered the courtroom on May 25. He stated that he, Wendell Phillips, and Theodore Parker all spoke to Burns before Judge Loring arrived and that Burns (having already essentially confessed to Suttle) had been reluctant to mount a defense. Dana claimed that, before any evidence was introduced, he had had a private conversation with Loring during which he asked Loring to call Burns to the desk and speak to him confidentially, and Loring had replied, "I intend to do so." Dana also asserted that Loring would have been justified in denying the initial request for a postponement on the ground that Burns had stated he did not desire to actively defend himself. "If Judge Loring had addressed [Burns] as all other judges address prisoners, across the bar, if [Loring] had not called [Burns] to him, and in a manner and tone at once kind and assuring urged a defence upon him, if he had not caught at a slight intimation of assent, I do not believe there would have been a defence at all." In addition, Dana emphasized that only Loring's intervention with Marshal Freeman made it possible for Phillips and Grimes to visit Burns during the trial and that Loring had acted at Grimes's request in trying to facilitate the purchase of Burns's freedom during the course of the rendition hearing. Though conceding that Loring may have commented to Phillips about the strength of the evidence against Burns, Dana suggested that it would be wrong to base removal "on a single phrase, as to which there may have been some misapprehension, or a failure to express correctly what was in the speaker's mind." Finally, Dana rebutted the claim that Loring had given advance notice of his decision to Freeman, referring to a contemporaneous conversation in which Freeman had flatly denied receiving any such notice. In short, far from viewing Loring as acting hostilely toward Burns, Dana characterized Loring's handling of the rendition proceeding as unusually sensitive to Burns's situation.

Dana then turned to the claim that Loring should be removed because he had first ordered Burns arrested and then ruled against him in the rendition proceeding. Disputing Phillips's assertion that these actions were, on their face, inconsistent with the policies embodied in the Personal Liberty Law of 1843, Dana emphasized both the language of the statute and the defeat of efforts to extend its prohibitions to the 1850 Fugitive Slave Act in both 1850 and 1852. Dana also observed that no one had suggested that George Ticknor Curtis's service as a commissioner in the proceedings involving Shadrach Minkins and Thomas Sims was inconsistent with his position as a state judge.

The specifics of Loring's decision posed a far more complex problem for Dana, who had been harshly critical of the decision at the time it was rendered. He began by asserting, "you would not remove [a judge] for a wrong decision. It must have been one so clearly wrong as to show him beyond doubt unfit for the judgeship of an inferior court, or to show corruption, or wilful error." Dana then observed that although "a decided preponderance of opinion at the Bar" believed that Loring had erred, at the very least, "one sound lawyer, who has distinguished himself by opposition to the Fugitive Slave Act," viewed the rendition decision as "inevitable." Thus, even though, in Dana's opinion, the decision was clearly wrong, he contended that it could not be characterized as beyond the bounds of reasonableness.

Turning once again to a contemporaneous entry in his own journal, Dana discussed the forces that might have predisposed Loring to reach his decision. In Dana's view:

> Judge Loring decided wrong — not from any corrupt motive, but from causes partly psychological, and partly accidental. This was a case admitting of, and to some extent requiring new applications or developments of fundamental principles, and Judge Loring has none of those strong instincts in favor of justice and humanity, which . . . have gradually changed the jurisprudence of England from a system of tyranny to a system of liberty; and the habit and associations of years, as well as his natural character, have led him to look chiefly at interests of property, and the preservation of quiet and ease.

Dana then explicitly attributed the decision to the baleful influence of Webster, Curtis, and their allies. While sharply rebuking Phillips and his allies for suggesting that Loring may have believed his position as commissioner was in jeopardy if he ruled in favor of Burns, Dana observed:

> Judge Loring had grown up under the shadow of Mr. Webster and Judge Shaw; he held their opinions . . . and the opinions of his friends, Judge Curtis and Judge Sprague, in the highest respect. He was a man to receive the opinions, and be much governed by the influences about him. He did not bring to the cause the high instincts of liberty and justice, the original power, the independence which the cause required.

Based on this tepid assessment of Loring's ability and character, Dana urged that he not be removed from office. At the same time,

Dana pressed the state legislature to pass a new personal liberty law that would explicitly ban state judges from serving as commissioners under the Fugitive Slave Act of 1850. By passing such a statute, Dana reasoned, the legislature could explicitly put judges in Loring's position on notice that, in the future, they could not both hold office in Massachusetts and participate in the enforcement of the federal statute.

After Dana completed his argument, Wendell Phillips rose to give a rebuttal. Phillips sarcastically asserted that, according to Dana, "the only moderate, judicious, dispassionate and white-robed citizen of the Commonwealth [during the Burns proceedings] was Edward Greely Loring; the only man that obeyed the law honestly, the only man that did his duty kindly, generously, conscientiously, and above suspicion was Edward Greely Loring." Otherwise, the rebuttal was largely a recapitulation of the points Phillips had made on February 20. Amid loud cheering for Phillips, the March 5 hearing was adjourned.

Without further hearings, on March 22 a majority of the committee produced a report arguing that Loring should be removed from office. Joined by Senator O. W. Albee, who chaired the committee, and Representatives James W. Stone, Elijah E. Knowles, and Oliver Warner, the report described the appropriate occasions for removal in sweeping terms:

> [An] individual holding office may not be guilty of crime, gross immorality or official misbehavior, so as to be liable to removal for such cause on trial and to judgment on impeachment, and yet, from gross or rash measures, or loathsomeness of person, or general offensiveness to the community, or from loss of the public confidence, ought to be removed by address.

After recounting in detail the legislative history of the removal provision, the majority report largely tracked the arguments made by Phillips. The report concluded that by detaining Burns, Loring had, at the very least, acted contrary to the "spirit and intent" of the Personal Liberty Law of 1843; that Loring had acted against the weight of the evidence in the rendition proceeding; that his statements to Phillips and his participation in the effort to purchase Burns's freedom indicated that he had prejudged the case; and that, by allowing the trial to be held with soldiers present, he had "outrage[d] the sense of the people."

The majority report also sought to turn a portion of Dana's argument against Loring. Noting Dana's suggestion that Loring "brought certain instincts from birth and education, and surrounding influences, certain associations and predilections which carried him inevitably to [his] decision," and that he lacked "strong instincts of *liberty* and *justice*," the report asked, "is a man, thus biased by education, association and surrounding influences as free, impartial and independent as the lot of humanity will admit?" It then asserted that the "Committee had always supposed that Massachusetts required her judges to bring instincts to the bench favorable to *liberty* and *justice* and not against them." Shortly thereafter the majority summed up the essence of its argument:

> The people . . . look on it as sinful and criminal to volunteer [to enforce the Fugitive Slave Act]. They cannot respect those who do it. They loathe to see or approach him who has received the price of his brother as they do the executioner, and cannot bear to see him in any office of honor or trust within the gift of Massachusetts.

Three members of the committee dissented from the majority report. Senator Bradford K. Pierce and Representative Erasmus Gould concurred in a brief statement that asserted, "no evidence has been offered to show that the decision in [the Burns case] was corrupt, or that, as a Commissioner [Loring] did not act in accordance with his own convictions of right," and that, while the sentiment of Massachusetts was against the enforcement of the Fugitive Slave Act, "both the forensic and popular sentiment, was not of so unmistakable a character as to assure him that, in sitting upon the case, he would sacrifice the confidence of those that appeared in his court." They concluded with an expression of concern for the independence of the judiciary and an expression of "reluctance in making one man, however objectionable his course may now be esteemed, a sacrifice for the sins of others . . . even for the benefit of a good cause."

Representative George H. Devereux sounded a similar note. He argued that, out of respect for the independence of the judiciary, the removal power should not be exercised in "any case other than of clear, unquestionable, self-evident deficiency or incompatibility, either physical, moral, or intellectual." Against this background, while condemning the Fugitive Slave Act itself as "repulsive and . . . odious," Devereux opposed removal because, in his view, the evidence did not demonstrate that Loring had been guilty of "wilful perversion of right or dereliction from duty."

At this point, the proceedings took an unusual turn. On April 2 Dana wrote a letter to the committee, asserting that he had requested that Leonard Grimes be called to corroborate his account of Loring's conduct of the hearing, but he had been assured by both Albee and Stone that Grimes's testimony was unnecessary because the committee would base its decision not on this issue but rather on the general question of whether Loring had acted inappropriately by enforcing the Fugitive Slave Act. Since the majority report had, in fact, relied extensively on the claim that Loring had conducted the hearing unfairly, Dana threatened to make these conversations public unless the committee took action to remedy the problem. Both Albee and Stone insisted that Dana had overstated the nature of their assurances and that he was at fault for failing to press harder to have Grimes called as a witness. Nonetheless, the committee decided to summon a number of witnesses to answer questions on April 3.

Grimes was the first witness to appear, and Dana was no doubt less than pleased with the overall tenor of his testimony. Grimes confirmed that Loring spoke to Burns in a "kindly and friendly" manner at the initial hearing, but he also took Loring to task for failing to meet him Monday morning as promised after the failed attempt to buy Burns's freedom on Saturday and for ruling against Burns after assuring Grimes that "if any doubts could be raised, [Burns] should have the benefit of them."

Grimes was followed by Henry Ware, an attorney who had attended the Burns hearings beginning on Monday, May 29. Though suggesting that he disagreed with the result, Ware described Loring's conduct of the proceedings as "deliberate, fair and courteous, unusually so for a slave commissioner, and much more than I or any other person had reason to expect in such a trial." He stated that Loring "weighed the testimony with due deliberation" and noted, "compared with the usual course of criminal trials in this State, to the mind of a person unbiased either by social or political feelings, his conducting the trial was entirely satisfactory." Ware did, however, comment that it was "not customary for Massachusetts Judges to sit surrounded by armed men within the courtroom," and when asked, he opined that Loring could have ordered the armed men to leave. Ware was immediately followed by Dana, who reappeared at the committee's request and, under questioning, essentially recapitulated his earlier argument.

The April 3 hearing ended with testimony from Charles Ellis, Theodore Parker, and Wendell Phillips, all of whom remained unremittingly hostile to Loring. Parker stated flatly that Loring "used all the advantages of his position to the detriment of Mr. Burns [and] went out of his way repeatedly, on almost every opportunity, to oppress the man before him." Ellis asserted that Loring's conduct had been "illegal and unjust." In addition, although Ellis could not state from personal knowledge that Loring had given Freeman advance notice of the decision to return Burns, "a variety of circumstances . . . leave no doubt in my mind that the Commissioner's decision was known [in advance]."

But perhaps the most striking feature of the testimony of this group of witnesses was their willingness to challenge Richard Henry Dana's account of his own actions and attitudes during the rendition hearing. Dana had quoted an entry from his journal that described Loring's conduct of the hearing as "considerate and humane," but Parker reported that, during the hearing itself, Dana had consistently characterized that conduct as "atrocious." Even more remarkably, Phillips disputed Dana's claim that he had had a private discussion with Loring in which the latter agreed to encourage Burns to mount a defense. Phillips assured the committee that "I do not question [Dana's] veracity, but only his memory," yet he testified that "if [Dana] had any information, such as he now swears to, from Judge Loring, neither his words nor his conduct show[ed] any hint of it. I cannot imagine that it can be true that he had that information . . . without informing us of it." Phillips continued, "when I first entered the room, he gave us to understand that he had made one ineffectual effort to arrest the trial."

After considering the additional testimony, the committee resubmitted its report with only minor alterations on April 4. Floor debates on the removal effort quickly began in the state house of representatives. The discussions featured impassioned rhetoric from both supporters and opponents of removal. For example, after discussing in detail the legal issues raised by the removal effort, John L. Swift of Boston concisely summarized the basic thrust of the removal movement, declaring that removal "will, in the most dignified and imperative manner, express the hatred, the indignation, and the condemnation which Massachusetts has for the institution of human slavery," and Charles W. Slack asserted that Loring "had . . . covered himself all over with infamy by his participation in these slave catching atrocities." Opponents were no less forceful in their denunciation of the removal movement. Bradford K. Pierce complained that "there is an insane cry for a victim and [the advocates of removal] hold that nothing short of a victim will produce the requisite impression here, at Washington and throughout the country." Geroge Read argued that "Judge Loring's removal will prove disastrous to the [cause of] antislavery reform, not only in Massachusetts, but throughout the country, and will be another example of the injury done by extreme measures to the cause of freedom throughout the country."

Opponents bolstered their critiques with allegations of unfairness. Some continued to insist that Loring had not had adequate notice that his participation in the Burns rendition would lead to the loss of his probate judgeship. For example, Eben Kimball insisted that "before Mr. Loring should be expelled from office, he ought to have some tangible expression of the people of this State" that state law prohibited such conduct. Seeking to address such concerns, J. M. S. Williams introduced an amendment in the form of a statute that would have prohibited state officials from holding the office of federal fugitive slave commissioner and also declared that any official who continued to act as a commissioner ten days after passage of the statute "shall be deemed to have afforded sufficient cause for removal, by address . . . and shall accordingly forthwith be removed."

This proposal was completely unacceptable to most supporters of removal by address. On April 13 James W. Stone outlined the reasons for their objections. Stone argued that the Williams proposal was an ex post facto law and unconstitutionally interfered with the legislature's discretion to determine whether removal was appropriate. But, more fundamentally, he asserted that if the Williams amendment were adopted, "it . . . will make every one of the slave hunters, from Maine to Texas, rejoice; will prevent the question respecting the removal of

Judge Loring to be taken upon its merits, [and] the main object which it is desirable to accomplish." In Stone's view, that object was "the prevention, in the future of any extradition of alleged fugitive slaves from the soil of Massachusetts; and especially, that it shall [not] be done by a Massachusetts judge, nor in direct violation of the right to trial by jury and of the privileges secured by the writ of *habeas corpus* and personal replevin." He contended that "[after] the transformation of a human being into a chattel . . . by a judge, and in neglect of that right, *great reasons of State* demand his removal." A narrow majority of his colleagues apparently agreed with these sentiments; on April 13 the amendment was defeated by a vote of 184–153. Efforts to allow Loring to resign voluntarily were rejected by similar margins, as were other proposed amendments. On April 14 the house voted to endorse removal by a vote of 206–111.

The opponents of removal still held out hope that the state senate would reach a different conclusion. However, the upper house proved no more sympathetic to Loring's cause. Noted abolitionist William Lloyd Garrison had been invited to observe the proceedings, and on April 25, with him looking on approvingly, the senate voted to concur with the house by a margin of 27–11.

Commentators who were strongly committed to the antislavery movement were predictably exultant. For example, immediately after the votes were counted, abolitionist Henry C. Wright exclaimed, "Thank God! The *State* has begun to move. She has taken *one* practical step against slavery." Soon thereafter, the *New York Independent* cheered that the vote in the two houses "shows that the people may be safely trusted where great interests of law, of justice, and humanity are involved, and that judicial tyranny is [not] tolerable in Massachusetts."

Not surprisingly, more conservative elements had a quite different reaction. For example, the day after the vote, the *Advertiser* bitterly asserted that "yesterday was a dark day for Massachusetts. The Senate . . . to which we looked for a rebuke to the fanaticism that has pervaded the House, prove[d] itself to have been quite as badly infected with the inania." The equally conservative *Boston Chronicle* similarly averred that, "prompted by sheer malice and love of mischief," the state legislature had voted to remove "a Judge who has been blameless and upright in his magistracy."

Loring's fate now rested with Governor Henry Gardner. In contemplating the removal address, Gardner may well have considered its potential implications for national politics as well as purely local concerns. The Know-Nothing Party was facing the first major test of its strength in the South in the Virginia gubernatorial election. Thomas S. Flournoy, the Know-Nothing candidate, was being harshly criticized by Henry A. Wise, his Democratic opponent, for his association with the Massachusetts party, which Wise characterized as a hotbed of "free soilism and abolitionism." Gardner himself was frequently cited by Wise and his supporters as being an apostle of the radical antislavery cause. Gardner must have been aware that Wise would seize on a decision to remove Loring as a vindication of this critique.

Against this background, Gardner refused to acquiesce in Loring's removal. On May 10 Gardner sent an official message to the speaker of the state house of representatives outlining the reasons for his decision. While conceding that "the tenor of the language of the Constitution seems to authorize [removal] in every case and without reasons given," Gardner observed, "if [this] be the meaning of [the removal provision] all sections of the Constitution referring to impeachment of Judges are superfluous." Relying heavily on what he characterized as the views of John Quincy Adams, Gardner contended that removal by address was proper only in cases in which the "dispensation of Providence . . . makes [judges], without criminality, incompetent to perform properly the duties of their office."

Gardner then argued that, even assuming the power of removal by address was not limited by the state constitution, Loring should not be removed. Raising the specter of a regime under which judges, like minor officials, would be removed with each change in the political complexion of the government, Gardner noted that Loring had neither committed any crime nor ignored his duties as a probate judge, and also observed that the legislature had twice failed to pass statutes that would have explicitly barred judges from acting as commissioners under the Fugitive Slave Act of 1850. In Gardner's opinion, removing Loring simply because his decision "shocked the popular sentiment of Massachusetts" was inconsistent with the principle that judges are required to follow the law, however unpopular. Crediting Dana's characterization of Loring's conduct of the rendition hearing as considerate and humane, Gardner brushed aside the claim that Loring should be removed simply because his decision in the Burns case was erroneous, noting that "such an impracticable and dangerous policy would lead to a daily removal" of judges from lower courts. Finally, in response to the argument that removal was appropriate because Loring "did not act up to the convictions of the people of Massachusetts concerning the constitutionality of [the Fugitive Slave Act]," Gardner noted that the support of Massachusetts politicians had been critical to the statute's passage only five years before, and that it would be unfair to punish Loring simply because the political winds had changed direction.

Gardner's decision was greeted with a twenty-one-gun salute on the Boston Common and by favorable comment from a variety of newspapers throughout the country. Predictably, Southern commentators were effusive in their praise. The *Daily South Carolinian* declared, "[Gardner's] heroic *acts* . . . stand out in bold relief . . . a beautiful contrast to the black fanaticism which pervades the body politic of his State," and the *Fayetteville Observer* stated, "we are happy to find that the authorities in Massachusetts are not *all* traitors and madmen." They were joined by a number of their Northern counterparts. The *New York Observer and Chronicle* praised Gardner for having the "firmness to resist the fanaticism and radicalism of the Legislature," while the conservative *National Intelligencer* asserted that Gardner had shown "moral courage unequaled by any other that occurs to us in the history of our government" and the *New York Times* averred that the removal of Loring "would have established a precedent in the highest degree dangerous to the integrity of the Judiciary and threatening to the stability of our institutions."

The radical antislavery press was understandably less pleased. Apparently implying that Gardner's decision was aimed at the Virginia electorate, the *Worcester Spy* railed that Gardner's action "detaches him from the support of his own fellow citizens of Massachusetts [and] attaches him to the proslavery citizens of Virginia," and *Frederick Douglass' Paper* declared that "such a Governor is [not] fit to control the interests of a free people."

Many antislavery legislators were equally irate. Representative Charles W. Slack contended that Gardner had violated the state constitution by not consulting with his executive council prior to reaching a decision. Although Gardner claimed that he was required to consult the council only when taking positive action — in this case, actually removing Loring — Slack moved that the legislature request a report from the council itself on the issue. However, this motion failed by a vote of 150–71.

Although the defeat of Slack's motion ended the formal inquiries into Gardner's decision not to remove Loring in 1855, Loring's status remained a bone of contention in Massachusetts politics for nearly three more years. Gardner's message left open the possibility that Loring could be removed if the state legislature explicitly made the office of probate judge inconsistent with service as a federal commissioner under the Fugitive Slave Act. The legislature almost immediately accepted this invitation as part of a much broader revision of the Massachusetts personal liberty law and thereby paved the way for Loring's removal.

CHAPTER II

The Personal Liberty Law of 1855 and the Removal of Edward Loring

In addition to pressing for the removal of Edward Loring, the antislavery forces sought to prevent a repeat of the successful rendition of Anthony Burns by strengthening the Massachusetts personal liberty law. The Massachusetts legislature had been working on such a revision at the same time it was considering the removal issue. Hearings were held before the Joint Standing Committee on Federal Relations during February 1855, and that committee reported a bill on April 25. The state senate passed the bill on May 14, and the house of representatives adopted an amended version five days later. The senate quickly agreed to the amendments, and the bill was sent to Governor Gardner on May 20, only ten days after he had declined to remove Loring. After consulting with the Supreme Judicial Court and the state attorney general, Gardner vetoed the bill on May 21, asserting that it unconstitutionally infringed on federal authority. Nonetheless, the bill became law the same day when the legislature overturned the veto by the staggering margins of 229–76 in the house and 31–3 in the senate.

The Massachusetts statute was the most radical and comprehensive personal liberty law ever adopted. Claimants with alleged slaves in custody were barred from state property, and the statute required state judges to order a jury trial whenever an alleged fugitive petitioned for a writ of habeas corpus. Claimants bore the burden of proof at such trials, but they were forbidden to offer oral testimony establishing their claims. Instead, the right to service could be established only by the testimony of at least two credible witnesses who had no material interest in the claimant's cause. Claimants who failed to provide the necessary evidence might be subject to fines and imprisonment under the statute's antikidnapping sections. In addition, Massachusetts lawyers were forbidden to represent claimants, and volunteer militiamen faced fines for protecting claimants from physical violence.

Other sections of the statute were aimed at the precise situation Loring had faced when he presided over the Burns hearing. Section 9 barred officeholders in Massachusetts from issuing warrants for fugitives or granting removal certificates. Section 10 permanently disqualified those who violated section 9 from their offices and honors, and section 12 provided that a refusal to resign a position as a slave commissioner would henceforth be deemed an adequate ground for either impeachment or removal.

Although the tenor of the personal liberty law infuriated both Southerners and conservative Northerners, none of these provisions was ever tested in court. Even before the passage of the statute, in the wake of the violence surrounding the rendition of both Thomas Sims and Anthony Burns, only a very brave or foolhardy Southerner would have attempted to recover a fugitive slave in Massachusetts after 1854. The draconian nature of the personal liberty law was simply the icing on the cake; there was no recorded effort to seize a fugitive slave in the commonwealth in the late 1850s.

However, two related sections of the new law became the focus of the ongoing struggle over the status of Edward Loring. Section 13 prohibited any person empowered to act as a slave commissioner from holding any state office, and section 14 provided that any state judge who continued to hold the position of commissioner in the federal courts for more than ten days following passage of the statute would be subject to removal by either impeachment or address. On its face, these provisions, clearly designed with Loring in mind, gave him a simple choice — either resign his post as commissioner or face losing his probate judgeship.

But at the same time, sections 13 and 14 were condemned as unconstitutional by critics of the new statute. The *Daily Advertiser*, for example, observed that the state constitution itself listed the offices that were inconsistent with service in the state government, and the office of commissioner of the federal court was nowhere mentioned. Thus, the *Advertiser* complained, the personal liberty law was an "attempt to engraft upon the State Constitution a new provision, which is beyond [the legislature's] constitutional authority, and which must be entirely inoperative."

Against this background, Loring ignored the new statute, retaining both his state and federal positions. However, this decision did not immediately bring the reaction one might have expected, given the passionate debates over his status in early 1855. Instead, the timing of his removal was dictated by the dynamics of the political struggle between the Republicans and the Know-Nothings in the mid-1850s.

One of the complicating features of this struggle was a rift over slavery that emerged in the Know-Nothing Party when the grand council of the order convened in Philadelphia on June 5, 1855. Southern Know-Nothings came to the convention smarting from the defeat of Thomas Flournoy in the Virginia gubernatorial election, a defeat the Southerners blamed on Henry Wise's success in linking Flournoy to "the fools and fanatics in the Legislature of Massachusetts" who identified themselves as Know-Nothings. Southerners were further dismayed when, during the meeting of the council, Free-Soiler John P. Hale of New Hampshire was elected to the U.S. Senate with the support of the Know-Nothings in the New Hampshire legislature. Thus, Southern council members attending the Philadelphia convention became determined to purge their party from what they saw as the taint of abolitionism. Conversely, Henry Wilson was equally determined to have antislavery language included in the party platform.

The climactic struggle came after the majority of the platform committee reported a provision declaring that "existing [federal] laws" on slavery should be viewed as a "final and conclusive settlement," thereby implicitly endorsing both the Kansas-Nebraska Act and the Fugitive Slave Act. The majority plank also denied that Congress had the power to legislate on the issue of slavery in the territories or to deny admission to a state because the state constitution allowed slavery and asserted that any effort to abolish slavery in the District of Columbia would be a violation of the "spirit and intention" of the compact by which Maryland had ceded that territory to the federal government. A minority proposal called for restoration of the Missouri Compromise and demanded that Congress not admit any slave states formed from the area north of the Missouri Compromise line, while a more neutral resolution simply stated that the issue of slavery was beyond the purview of the Know-Nothing order. When the council adopted the majority, pro-slavery resolution on June 13, the Northern delegates bolted from the convention. The following day the Northerners met and adopted their own platform, which featured a plank that called for the restoration of the Missouri Compromise and demanded that the voting rights of antislavery residents of Kansas be protected and that both Kansas and Nebraska be admitted as free states.

Both Henry Wilson and Henry Gardner attended the national council, joined their Northern colleagues in walking out after adoption of the pro-slavery platform, and participated in drafting the platform adopted by the erstwhile Northern delegates. However, their perspectives on the Know-Nothing Party and its disruption differed markedly. Wilson's association with the Know-Nothing movement had never been anything more than a convenient device for advancing his antislavery political agenda. Thus, he seized on the sectional split in the party as an opportunity to press for fusion among all antislavery politicians—a movement that soon found its voice in the nascent Republican Party.

Gardner, by contrast, was far less committed to the antislavery movement in either principle or practice. When the Whigs disintegrated, the Know-Nothing Party had simply become his most obvious alternative political home. In addition, he saw the party as a vehicle for the advancement of his national political ambitions. Indeed, he had come to Philadelphia hoping to be elected president of the national order, and he endorsed the minority, antislavery platform plank only after that ambition had been thwarted. Even after the schism, Gardner sought to preserve the Northern wing of the party as an independent political organization whose basic ideology was not viewed as solely or even primarily antislavery in nature. Thus, Gardner was instrumental in preventing a call for fusion from being included in the platform adopted in Philadelphia by the Northern Know-Nothings.

The conflict between these two visions of the future of the antislavery movement was a dominant feature of Massachusetts politics for the next several years. On August 22, antislavery politicians of all stripes met in Boston and planned both a mass meeting and a nominating convention to be held in Worcester on September 20 to launch the Republican Party in Massachusetts. The call for the convention did not mention either Loring specifically or the issue of fugitive slaves generally. Instead, the call was directed simply at those who were "opposed to the extension of slavery." The focus on the issue of slavery in the territories reflected a belief that, to succeed on a national level, the newly formed party would have to appeal to voters who did not care about the issue of fugitive slaves and had no desire to have their communities become refuges for such fugitives.

Nonetheless, the question of whether Loring should be removed was not entirely ignored during the September 20 proceedings. At the convention, Henry Gardner sought to subordinate the fusion movement to the antislavery Know-Nothings by obtaining the Republican nomination for governor. Gardner was supported by a plurality of the delegates to the convention on the first ballot but did not receive the majority necessary to receive the nomination. Antislavery veteran J. Q. A. Griffin then vigorously attacked Gardner at the mass meeting, focusing in part on Gardner's refusal to remove Loring and veto of the personal liberty law. By contrast, speaking to the convention itself, Dana argued that Gardner's candidacy should be rejected not because of his treatment of Loring but because he was not truly committed to the fusion movement. Against this background, on the next ballot the convention passed over Gardner in favor of Julius Rockwell, a former U.S. senator. In support of Rockwell's candidacy, the convention adopted a platform that once again focused solely on opposition to the expansion of slave territory. Gardner subsequently ran on an antislavery platform as a Know-Nothing and defeated Rockwell, Democrat Edward Beach, and unreconstructed Cotton Whig Samuel Whalley to gain a second term as governor.

With Gardner in office and the emotions aroused by the Burns rendition no longer quite so raw, the issue of Loring's fate temporarily receded into the background. In 1856 the state legislature focused its attention on Gardner's ultimately unsuccessful effort to have the personal liberty law repealed in whole or in part. However, in late April the *New York Tribune* sought to revive the removal campaign. The *Tribune* observed that Gardner's explanation for refusing to remove Loring in 1855 had focused in part on the lack of a clear statutory violation and that Loring was now violating the personal liberty law by retaining his position as a probate judge. Elaborating on this position, the *Tribune*'s Boston correspondent sought to turn Loring's legalistic defense of his actions in the Burns case against him, asserting:

[Loring] has been living for a year in the most flagrant and impudent disobedience to the laws of the State, and common self-respect and ordinary resentment of an insult should prompt the legislature to give him the effectual kick [in the] behind, which Governor Gardner intercepted last year and hindered from sending him sprawling into the street. [Loring's] Webster Whig friends could make no objection now, when they remember that "law is to be obeyed, however unpleasant it may be, when it is law."

Perhaps reminded by the *Tribune*, the *Liberator* rejoined the fray, soliciting its readers to sign petitions calling for Loring's removal based on his violation of the statute. But with the 1856 session drawing to a close and Gardner almost certainly remaining opposed to removal in any event, state legislators had no stomach for revisiting such an explosive issue. With most senators not even participating, by a margin of 12–8, the state senate refused to refer the removal petitions to the appropriate committee, choosing instead to postpone consideration of the matter until the 1857 term.

In the interim, Henry Gardner successfully navigated the treacherous political waters swirling around the presidential election of 1856 to gain a third one-year term as governor. After his efforts to win a place on a national ticket or to position himself to succeed Charles Sumner in the U.S. Senate in 1857 proved unavailing, Gardner was faced with the prospect of another strong Republican challenge in the gubernatorial race. Gardner defused this possibility by threatening to run on an antislavery Know-Nothing ticket in the presidential election, creating the likelihood of splitting the antislavery vote and causing the defeat of Republican presidential nominee John Frémont in Massachusetts. Seeking to forestall this eventuality, mainstream Republicans agreed not to nominate a candidate for governor in return for Gardner's pledge to support their presidential ticket. Although a small number of radical Republicans repudiated the agreement and nominated Josiah Quincy for governor on the so-called Honest Man's ticket, Gardner triumphed easily in the election. At the same time, Republicans established clear majorities in both houses of the state legislature.

Gardner's third term was marked by the resumption of concerted efforts to remove Loring from the probate court. Although passions surrounding the issue had cooled somewhat, in March 1857 the legislature was once more presented with numerous petitions calling for Loring's removal. However, unlike the earlier petitions, which had focused on Loring's conduct in the Burns rendition proceeding, the

1857 petitions emphasized Loring's failure to comply with the terms of the Personal Liberty Law of 1855, which required him to choose between his probate judgeship and his position as commissioner of the federal district court. Once again the petitions were referred to the Joint Standing Committee on Federal Relations, whose membership now included Senators O. W. Albee and John M. Merrick and Representatives John Wells, Jonathan Swift, John E. Ward, Richard Ramsdell, and Henry Bradley.

Loring quickly responded in writing to the removal petitions. Relying on the express views of both Governor Gardner and Attorney General Clifford, Loring argued that the personal liberty law was unconstitutional. Noting that he had taken an oath to support the state constitution, Loring declared, "the Magistrate who furthers by obedience or otherwise, directly or indirectly, and in any degree, an unconstitutional law violates his duty and is guilty of perjury." From this perspective, he argued, his failure to resign not only was unexceptionable but also "directly fulfilled[ed] [his] duty as a citizen and a magistrate, to the constitution and people of Massachusetts." Loring contended that his removal by petition would threaten judicial independence, asserting, "it is the meaning and purpose of the constitution, that the official action of Judicial officers shall be inquired into, only on impeachment, before the appointed tribunal and according to the due forms of law; that there is no other protection for the Judiciary against popular excitements, the dominance of party and the legislation it fashions."

On March 24 the supporters of removal made their case in a hearing before the committee. William I. Bowditch began by reiterating the view that the power to remove by petition and address was unlimited and harshly criticizing Loring's actions in the Burns rendition proceedings. He then disputed Loring's claim that section 14 of the personal liberty law was unconstitutional and concluded by declaring, "we cannot say to Judge Loring that he shall not be a United States Commissioner, but we may say and ought to say, that he shall not be a Judge of Probate at the same time." Picking up on the same theme, John N. Brown referred to Loring as a "public criminal" and stated, "the petitioners ask that the State shall vindicate itself. It is simply a question of whether the State shall bow to Judge Loring, or Judge Loring bow to the state." Appearing before the committee one week later, John A. Andrew reiterated this view, contending that "if it is the object of the legislature to make laws to be executed . . . the removal of Judge Loring is an inevitable exigency."

On Monday, April 20, John Wells delivered a majority report recommending against removal. Speaking for himself, Merrick, Ramsdell, and Bradley, Wells began by asserting that only the claim that Loring had violated section 14 should be considered in determining whether to remove the probate judge from his position. Though conceding that Loring's conduct in the Burns case had been discussed at the 1857 hearings, Wells observed that Loring's detractors had disavowed any intention to rely on that conduct as a basis for removal; therefore, Loring had had no real opportunity to address these concerns, and the majority argued that it would be unfair to rely on this ground to remove Loring.

Taking this narrow focus, Wells agreed with Loring that section 14 was unconstitutional. However, Wells's premises were quite different from Loring's. Wells had no difficulty in viewing the removal provision of the state constitution as unlimited in scope; in fact, he explicitly embraced that view. But at the same time, Wells contended that section 14 was unconstitutional because it was an attempt by the 1855 state legislature to unduly limit the discretion of subsequent bodies in considering the merits of removal petitions.

Speaking for himself and Ward, Albee — the only holdover from the 1855 committee that had called for Loring's removal — delivered a lengthy rebuttal to the majority report. In addition to arguing that section 14 was in fact constitutional, Albee charged Loring with hypocrisy in "follow[ing] his own feeling instead of standing law" after portraying himself as a "reverent disciple of the law" in his 1855 defense. Albee then recapitulated the litany of charges leveled against Loring for his actions in the Burns case and asserted that these actions also justified Loring's removal from office.

The state senate took up the issue on May 6. Arguing that the removal address should include a detailed indictment of Loring's treatment of Burns as well as follow the dictates of section 14, Albee asserted that in the rendition proceedings, Loring had "trampled under foot the moral sentiment of Massachusetts, and had set at naught her often expressed wishes." With respect to the section 14 issue, Albee reiterated the view that "Judge Loring [is] now acting in open defiance of the law, and dares the Legislature to remove him . . . either the dignity of the law must yield, or it must be maintained."

Merrick's response to this argument was twofold. First, emphasizing the fact that the removal petitions had focused only on Loring's violation of section 14, Merrick reiterated the majority's view that only that issue could properly be considered. Second, while conceding that the legislature could have prohibited Loring from simultaneously holding the positions of probate judge and U.S. commissioner *before* he had accepted both commissions, Merrick contended that it was unjust and unconstitutional for the state legislature to "expel [Loring] from office by the imposition of new conditions, inconsistent with those under which the office was bestowed and accepted." Invoking the need to preserve judicial independence, Merrick argued that removing Loring would set a precedent "which might hereafter be followed by parties or partisans zealous to get rid of a competent [judge] on party grounds; or to expose the Judiciary of the Commonwealth to popular excitement."

Merrick's argument was to no avail. By a vote of 20–15, the senate agreed to adopt an address along the lines suggested by Albee. Then, in an apparent nod to moderates, the senators voted 25–12 to delete all references to Loring's actions in the rendition proceedings, other than the simple claim that by agreeing to act as a slave commissioner he had defied "the moral sentiments of the people of Massachusetts."

The state house of representatives took up the proposed address to the governor on May 19. Although asserting that Loring's actions in the rendition proceeding had been "warped by his prejudices and sympathies," Ward based his support of the senate address solely on Loring's violation of section 14. Other supporters of removal couched their arguments in terms that were reminiscent of the 1855 debate. For example, disclaiming any reliance on the section 14 argument, Swift complained that Loring had "abused the power placed in his hands, and insulted the majesty of the Commonwealth," and stated that "his rulings in [the Burns case] were as tyrannical and cold-blooded as any that ever fell from the lips of any judge." John Wells and Charles Hale, by contrast, reiterated the view that Loring's removal would threaten judicial independence, with Wells declaring that removal would "be applying a greater evil to cure a lesser evil" and Hale asserting that removal would initiate a regime in which judges served at the pleasure of the dominant party. Despite these arguments, the address was overwhelmingly adopted by the house by a vote of 210–69.

The ongoing effort to remove Loring generated a variety of responses from the Massachusetts press. For example, whereas the *Advertiser* voiced its support for Loring's position, insisting that section 14 was "palpably unconstitutional" because "it is not within the province of the legislature to make a definition of judicial misbehavior," the *Boston Daily Bee* supported the removal effort, contending that if Loring were entitled to ignore section 14 simply because of his personal belief that the statute was unconstitutional, others were equally justified in resisting enforcement of the Fugitive Slave Act because they believed it to be unconstitutional.

The case continued to attract national attention as well. Both the *Daily Chronicle and Sentinel* of Augusta, Georgia, and the *National Intelligencer* approvingly quoted a passage from the *Boston Journal* that described the removal effort as "a singular instance of political zeal overreaching itself and losing all by grasping too much." Similarly, the *Savannah Daily Morning News* cited the removal vote as evidence of the progress of "fanaticism" in Massachusetts.

With opinion thus divided, on June 1 Henry Gardner informed the legislature that he remained unwilling to strip Loring of his probate judgeship. On July 1 Gardner provided a detailed account of the reasons for his decision. Gardner began by reiterating his view that the removal provision was intended to apply only to judges who had become incapacitated and were unable to properly discharge their duties for that reason. Though conceding that in his 1855 message he had recognized the legislature's authority to remove judges for plain violations of the law, Gardner asserted that he had been referring to the power to strip judges of their commission through the impeachment process. He then argued that section 14 of the personal liberty law was unconstitutional for two reasons – first, because it purported to limit the terms of judges in a manner not consistent with the state constitution, and second, because it was in essence an ex post facto law. Gardner also raised the standard of judicial independence, contending that if a judge's tenure could be limited by a provision such as section 14, judges could be removed "whenever party prejudice may demand, or party policy may dictate." Finally, Gardner expressed the belief that the removal issue would be addressed in the next gubernatorial election, averring that "the actions of party leaders, the unmistakable speeches of partisan orators, and the tone of a portion of the political press, conclusively indicate that the question is now to be taken from the halls of legislation and from Executive action, to be adjudicated by the votes of our citizens at the ensuing State election." Gardner concluded by stating that he had "unswerving faith that the conservative and intelligent verdict of my fellow citizens will sustain my views of public duty."

Gardner's supporters indeed made persistent efforts to deploy the removal issue in his campaign for reelection in 1857. His main competition in the race was Nathaniel P. Banks Jr., who apparently had no strong commitment to either nativism or the ideology of the antislavery movement. Nonetheless, Banks had a record of successfully straddling the nascent Republican Party and the Know-Nothings during the political upheaval of the mid-1850s.

After serving in the state house of representatives for four years, Banks was elected to Congress as a Democrat in 1852 and reelected as a Know-Nothing in 1854. After his reelection, Banks became the Republican candidate for Speaker of the House and, after a bitter struggle, was chosen for that post with substantial Know-Nothing support. In 1856, serving as a stalking horse for John Frémont, Banks was selected as the presidential nominee of the North American Party, a dissident group of Know-Nothings who had split with the national organization over the issue of slavery and the nomination of Millard Fillmore for president. Shortly after winning the North American Party nomination, Banks, following a prearranged plan, withdrew from the race, leaving Frémont with no competition for the antislavery vote.

In the Massachusetts gubernatorial contest of 1857, Banks became the nominee of both the North American and Republican parties. Much to the chagrin of some more radical Republicans, neither the party platform nor Banks himself made any explicit mention of the dispute over Judge Loring. Instead, Banks blandly asserted, "I have opposed with earnest the policy of the slave propagandists, and have endeavored . . . to defeat . . . measures, which were calculated, in my judgment, to substitute for toleration of negro bondage in the states where it now exists, its absolute dominion."

Gardner was the nominee of a coalition of dissident Know-Nothings and unreconstructed Whigs. Opposition to Loring's removal featured prominently in the campaign rhetoric of his supporters. Gardner himself disapprovingly noted that Banks had "said nothing about Judge Loring; nothing about sustaining the Judiciary of Massachusetts of Massachusetts under the constitution of Massachusetts." Similarly, observing that "what Mr. Banks will do is uncertain and undefined," George F. Hilliard declared, "every man in this state who . . . does not wish Judge Loring removed, is bound . . . to vote for Governor Gardner." Carrying the argument one step further and construing Banks's silence as support for removal, Robert C. Winthrop declared that he could not vote "for one . . . who places so low an estimate on the value of an independent judiciary, that he would . . . remove a state [judge] for a decision or decree, however unpalatable, which may have been given in the conscientious discharge of duty."

Despite the emphasis placed on the issue by Gardner's supporters, the fate of Edward Loring was not the central issue in Massachusetts in 1857. Instead, the election almost certainly turned on the economic development of the state. Voters clearly wanted a change in policy, and Banks won a comfortable plurality, receiving over 45 percent of the vote. Gardner was the choice of less than 30 percent of the electorate, and Democratic candidate Erasmus D. Beach received approximately 25 percent of the vote. Caleb B. Swan, the choice of the radical "Straight Republicans," ran far behind, with only 213 votes. The so-called American Republicans who supported Banks were even more dominant in the elections for the state legislature, winning more than two-thirds of the seats in the state house of representatives, with the remaining seats almost equally divided between Gardnerites and Democrats, and gaining an even larger proportion of seats in the state senate.

But like the Know-Nothings before them, the American Republicans were far from unified in their views on the appropriate treatment of Judge Loring. Seeking to place their stamp on the newly elected government, beginning in late 1857, radicals advocating Loring's removal pressed their cause with a vigor unmatched since the original removal campaign in 1855. An 1857 statute had placed stringent procedural requirements on petitions to the legislature. Nonetheless, by early 1858 the pro-removal forces had obtained more than 7,600 signatures on removal petitions.

The aggressive removal campaign created an awkward political problem for Banks, who had designs on the Republican presidential nomination in 1860. If he removed Loring, Banks ran the risk of alienating the conservative Republicans who opposed removal. However, by opposing the removal movement, Banks could render himself completely unacceptable to more radical Republicans, who might otherwise reluctantly acquiesce in his nomination.

Banks devised a clever solution to this dilemma. He introduced a plan to merge the probate courts with the insolvency court system, an unpopular institution that had been created in 1856. If passed by the legislature, this plan would have eliminated Loring's position, thus effectively removing him from office without naming him personally or passing judgment on either his actions in the Burns case or his decision not to honor section 14 of the personal liberty law. A correspondent to the *New York Times* observed, "in this way, an obnoxious officer will be shelved, and a vexatious matter . . . disposed of in a manner satisfactory to nearly the whole public."

However, this approach drew fire from a number of different quarters. Members of the radical antislavery faction continued to insist on an explicit condemnation of both Loring's actions in the rendition proceeding and his refusal to abide by the terms of section 14. These legislators and their supporters maneuvered to force legislative action on the removal petitions before the consolidation plan could be passed, rendering the petitions moot.

The situation was further complicated by the oratory of Democrat Caleb Cushing, who overtly took the position that the South was the wronged party in the sectional conflict—a viewpoint that had been conspicuously absent in the previous debates over Loring's removal. Before being returned to the state legislature in 1857 after a six-year absence, Cushing had a long and distinguished career in public service. From 1853 through 1857 he served as attorney general in the administration of Franklin Pierce and thus played a key role in devising and implementing the administration's policy during the rendition of Anthony Burns and its aftermath.

Like Banks, Cushing saw himself as a potential presidential candidate. But in a national Democratic Party increasingly dominated by the South, only a Northerner with a record of sympathy for Southern positions could realistically hope to gain the nomination. During the 1857 campaign Cushing complained that abolitionists had created a climate of "morbid jealousy, and even hatred of the people of the South" in Massachusetts, and he accused Banks and other moderate politicians of seeking to capitalize on these sentiments for political gain. In January 1858, after the victory of Banks and his allies in the election, Cushing characterized the removal effort as part of an abolitionist plan to control the state legislature and vowed to "contradict such false and arrogant dictatorship by kicking those insulting petitioners out of the house."

Wendell Phillips added fuel to the fire in a speech to the annual meeting of the Massachusetts Anti-Slavery Society on January 29. He suggested that the abolitionists controlled the removal process, asserting, "I met a Republican leader in . . . Boston, after the election of Mr. Banks . . . and asked what he supposed would be the effect of the vote on Judge Loring. 'We want to know what you want us to do,' he replied." The meeting then adopted a series of resolutions calling for Loring's removal and implicitly rejecting Banks's approach, declaring that "the people will not sanction or tolerate any measure whereby this issue shall be evaded, but will hold every Senator and Representative, to the strictest accountability in this case, together with the Governor and every member of his Council."

The blandishments of the Anti-Slavery Society did little to advance the cause of removal. Indeed, loathe to be tarred with the brush of abolitionism, some more moderate Republicans showed a notable lack of enthusiasm for aggressive action that singled out Loring. Thus, the Federal Relations Committee, chaired by moderate Republican Henry Vose of Springfield, refused to take jurisdiction over consideration of the removal petitions, as did the Probate and Chancery Committee led by antislavery stalwart John A. Andrew. Ultimately, both houses agreed to create a joint special committee to consider the issue, but the state senate did not appoint its committee members until late February. Although Andrew and Robert C. Pitman forced consideration of the removal petitions by the full house on February 18, the petitions were quickly tabled after a brief debate.

Cushing, in contrast, seized on the Phillips speech to extend his aggressive assault on the removal movement. In a February 21 speech on the house floor, Cushing argued that the petitions did not satisfy the legal requirements established in 1857 and noted that Phillips had proclaimed that a "whipped spaniel . . . should be the emblem of the state legislature." Cushing asserted that, by voting for removal, the house would be acting like a "whipped spaniel crouching at the feet of the Massachusetts Anti-Slavery Society" and would be admitting "that [the] pretension of the Anti-Slavery Society is true, that you are subject to its dictation, that what it commands is performed, that you do not sit here to act upon your own judgment, but [are] the humble registers of the edicts of the Massachusetts Anti-Slavery Society." Cushing was equally contemptuous of Banks's consolidation scheme, averring sarcastically:

> This House, whatever it does for the removal of Judge Loring, must be careful not to trouble [Banks's] prospects in the Middle States. It is therefore proposed to this legislature, that we shall ride rough-shod over the Constitution of the Commonwealth; that we shall trample upon the rights and interests of its respected public servants who now administer the judiciary of the Commonwealth, and all this, because it will be inconvenient if Judge Loring is fired at with cannon balls [as advocated by Phillips].

As the debate over removal continued, Banks's supporters in the legislature were making strenuous efforts to end the controversy through the adoption of his judicial consolidation plan. The consolidation bill was reported by the Senate Judiciary Committee on February 13 and came to the floor of the state house of representatives on March 1. With many members of the house absent, a coalition of Gardnerites, Democrats, and radical antislavery representatives was able to pass a motion (by a vote of 83–33) to postpone consideration of the consolidation bill until March 17.

The parliamentary maneuvering continued the next day in a much fuller, closely divided house. Amid discussions marked by bitter recriminations between those who wanted to vote directly on Loring's removal and those who favored using the consolidation bill to resolve the issue, the Banks forces initially succeeded in calling the bill from the table by a 103–98 margin. The anti-consolidationists then reversed this decision on a 101–99 vote, after which the decision to bring the bill to the floor was reinstated by a vote of 102–93. Following a failed motion to postpone consideration of the bill until March 16, a postponement until March 10 was agreed on.

March 2 also saw the first and only formal meeting of the joint committee created to consider the removal petitions. Despite the vigor with which the issue of removal was debated in the legislature and the newspapers, public interest in the fate of Edward Loring was clearly flagging; the hearing was much more sparsely attended than the raucous proceedings held in 1855. Once again, Loring did not appear in person but submitted a brief written statement reiterating his view that section 14 of the personal liberty law was unconstitutional. William Lloyd Garrison and Aaron Bradley appeared before the committee to urge removal; however, only Garrison's remarks were recorded.

Speaking on behalf of himself and a group of prominent abolitionists, Garrison's frustration over the previous failed removal efforts was palpable. Although he briefly recapitulated the theories on which removal was urged, Garrison also noted that the legislature had twice voted to remove Loring after extensive hearings and declared, "the time has gone by for hesitancy or doubt, for argument or procrastination. . . . The subject . . . requires no repetition of words, no new evidence, but only ACTION." Garrison disdained the approach advocated by Banks, contending instead that "this case [must] be met upon its merits, and by a direct vote; and not be superseded, or evaded, or jeopardized, by any other question." He declared that removal would "vindicate . . . the insulted majesty of the State, give heed to the voice of the people, and . . . confer upon the Legislature and the present State administration lasting honor, secure the public repose, and promote public justice." Soon after Garrison's presentation, Representative John W. Foster sought to derail the removal effort on the floor of the house by moving to seek the opinion of the Supreme Judicial Court on the issue, but this motion was overwhelmingly defeated by a vote of 198–28.

Against this background, the joint committee issued its report on May 9. By a 6–1 margin, the committee recommended that Loring be removed. Initially, the responsibility for preparing the majority report rested with Representative Joseph M. Churchill. However, after the tone of Churchill's draft proved too radical for some members of the majority, the task was reassigned to Senator William T. Davis.

The majority report began by defining the scope of the removal power in the broadest possible terms, asserting that "any reasons [other

than those that would warrant impeachment] which may seem sufficient, will justify removal by address." The report explicitly declined
to base the majority's position on section 14 of the personal liberty
law, except insofar as that provision reflected a more general view that
the duties of a probate court judge were inconsistent with those of a
commissioner of the federal district court. Instead, Davis argued that
the two commissions were inconsistent because Loring might be
forced to abandon or postpone the completion of his probate court
duties to fulfill the responsibilities of a federal commissioner. Davis
also hypothesized a situation in which Loring, in his capacity as a probate judge, might be called on to appoint a guardian for children
whose mother was a deceased fugitive slave, suggesting that Loring's
obligation to be their "protector and friend" would come into direct
conflict with his obligation as a commissioner to remand the children
to the service of the mother's master.

In his dissenting report, Gardnerite William Page made a number
of different points. First, Page argued that the petitions did not meet
the technical requirements established in 1857. In addition, he recapitulated many of the anti-removal points made by others, contending that use of the removal power should be limited to situations in
which a judge had become disabled and that the Fugitive Slave Act was
constitutional whereas the personal liberty law was unconstitutional.
Page also appealed to the concept of judicial independence, noting
that Loring had "faithfully and satisfactorily" performed the duties
of a probate judge.

The issuance of the committee report cleared the way for floor
action on the removal address. However, there was still the possibility that the consolidation bill, which was scheduled for action in the
house, would pass before the legislature could act. Therefore, when
the consolidation bill came up for consideration on March 10, pro-
removal representative Dexter C. Parker acted quickly to eliminate
this possibility, moving to table the orders of the day (which included
the consolidation bill), discharge the removal from the orders of the
day, and immediately consider the removal address. After the sound
defeat of Cushing's motion to recommit the address pending an investigation of possible impeachable offenses, debate on the matter was
postponed for a day at his request to allow him to prepare a speech.

On March 11, speaking before a crowded gallery, Cushing opened the debate over the removal issue. He began by asserting that the removal of Judge Loring was contrary to public sentiment and would plunge the state of Massachusetts into "the unfathomable gulf of disunion." Cushing then launched a starkly racist attack on the two men who had argued for removal before the committee, characterizing William Lloyd Garrison as representing "the monomania of negro idolatry" and, in a clear reference to Aaron Bradley, sneering that "there was, forsooth, a poor, half-demented man, who made upon me the impression of a man who suffered a great misfortune when he lost his master." More generally, Cushing analogized those who pressed for Loring's removal to the mob that had cried loudly for the crucifixion of Jesus Christ. Later, Cushing invoked the principle of judicial independence, contending that under the regime envisioned by the pro-removal forces, "judges are to depend on the shifting caprice of the sovereign, in the form of popular clamor." Cushing concluded his remarks by moving again to have the issue returned to the committee to determine whether Loring had committed any impeachable offense. That motion was soundly defeated by a margin of 130–44.

Representative Charles Hale of Boston, the editor of the *Daily Advertiser* who, by 1858, had associated himself with the Republican Party, also spoke against removal. However, the tone of his remarks was far less belligerent than Cushing's. Hale argued that if the personal liberty law was interpreted to mandate the removal of state judges who served simultaneously as federal commissioners, then the statute unconstitutionally limited the tenure of judges. Conversely, he contended that if the statute did *not* require removal, then it was simply irrelevant to the case against Loring. Hale also asserted that Loring could easily perform the duties of both offices and proclaimed, "it is prejudice that dictates [the removal] proceeding." Finally, Hale made a political argument, asserting that Loring's removal could divide the antislavery movement by alienating a significant number of voters who opposed the expansion of slavery, averring that "it is scarcely worthwhile in a matter of this kind to give weighty cause of offence to the large numbers of voters in Massachusetts who, while they agree in resisting the spread of slavery are nevertheless fundamentally opposed to the removal of Judge Loring."

On the last point, Hale found support from some Republicans who had hitherto supported removal. In 1858 the debate over removal took place against the background of the simultaneous effort of the Buchanan administration to have Kansas admitted to the Union as a slave state under the pro-slavery Lecompton constitution. Many Northern Democrats, led by Senator Stephen A. Douglas of Illinois, strongly opposed this effort, viewing the Lecompton constitution as the product of an illegitimate process. Some Republicans hoped to exploit the rift to recruit anti-Lecompton Democrats. One of the obstacles to this effort was the Democratic claim that the Republican Party was a radical movement — a perception that might be given greater credence by the removal of Loring. Thus, the *Springfield Republican*, which had strongly supported the removal movement since 1855, now proclaimed that "the removal of Judge Loring is waited for, and doubtless prayed for, by the pro-slavery party to be used [as evidence of radicalism] against the republicans in states where the national conflict is doubtful." Observing that Loring would, in any event, lose his position under the consolidation bill, the *Republican* contended that removal should be defeated to "contribute something to the common sacrifice of personal and party feeling that all the opponents of the [Buchanan] administration have got to make, in order to make that opposition effective and useful."

Despite this plea, most Republicans remained undeterred. John Andrew, for example, insisted that "there is no way to escape [removal] consistently with the preservation of our rights and our honor." Andrew characterized simultaneous service in the judicial branches of the federal and state governments as inconsistent with the basic principles of American federalism. Focusing more specifically on Loring's situation, Andrew described the conflict between the duties of a probate judge and those of a commissioner as "flagrant and direct." Andrew also proclaimed, "the people believe it to be inconvenient and unsafe that a man holding a judicial office . . . shall also hold an office that imperatively demands the performance of functions which are in conflict with the heart and conscience of the people." Robert Pitman was even more emphatic, challenging the opponents of removal

to say, whether a man who violates the law of the Commonwealth, and sets the Commonwealth at defiance not merely, but does it defiantly assuming upon his own private opinion of the constitutionality of a law to disobey it, not as a *martyr*, but as a man eating his master's bread and spurning both his wishes and demands and keeping his salary. — I put it to them to say, whether the insulted majesty of the Commonwealth does not demand some vindication at our hands?

The supporters of removal often linked their positions with attacks on the Fugitive Slave Act itself. Dexter Parker urged outright nullification, declaring, "if [the personal liberty law] violates the law of the country, the time has come when the States must interpret the Constitution for themselves." Andrew was only slightly less emphatic, declaring that, because African Americans were presumed to be free persons in Massachusetts, the courts would be forced to decide that the Fugitive Slave Act "cannot be the law in Massachusetts, for it strikes at all [the African Americans'] rights of manhood."

Ultimately, the overwhelming majority of house Republicans chose to support removal. Although opposed almost unanimously by Gardnerites and Democrats, on March 12 the removal address was adopted by a vote of 127–101, with Republicans supporting the motion by a 123–36 margin. The following day the consolidation bill passed in the house as well. However, before the bill could be considered by the senate, on March 17, with much less drama than in the house, the senate endorsed removal by a vote of 24–14.

With the consolidation bill not yet enacted into law, Banks could not avoid facing the removal issue directly. No doubt recognizing that a refusal to act against Loring would antagonize many Republicans, Banks signed the removal address on March 19. However, Banks's explanation for his decision was couched in extremely moderate language. While expressing the view that the removal power is "given without qualification and its exercise is intrusted solely to the discretion of the Legislature and executive branches of the government," Banks disclaimed any reliance on Loring's actions in the Burns rendition proceeding. Instead, Banks focused solely on Loring's refusal to abide by the terms of section 14 of the personal liberty law, declaring, "I entertain no doubt of the power of the Legislature to establish the incompatibility [of the offices of probate judge and U.S. commissioner] and . . . I consider its exercise [in this context] eminently wise and just." Banks then noted that, in justifying his refusal to honor the dictates of section 14, Loring "has reasserted his purpose and position, conscientiously, I have no doubt, in language which I cannot interpret otherwise than as manifesting a fixed resolution to disregard and in effect to nullify a statute provision of the Commonwealth. For this reason [alone] I have removed Edward Greely Loring from the office of [probate judge]." Banks further moderated the tone of his removal message by taking the opportunity to call for the repeal of some of the more sweeping provisions of the personal liberty law.

The transmission of Banks's message to the state house of representatives sparked a final sharp exchange between Cushing and Andrew. After Andrew moved to refer the governor's recommendations on alterations of the personal liberty law to a special committee, Cushing took the floor and declared, "those who have substituted a religion of hate for a religion of love, who in their love of the black race are actuated by demoniac hatred of the white race, have triumphed." He continued, "the sworn enemies of the Constitution have succeeded. . . . We have entered in that career of attack upon the institutions of the Union, the issue of which is known only to God. Judge Loring is to be the first sacrificed. Who is to be the next?" Andrew responded by praising Banks's "courage to vindicate the law of Massachusetts — the *constitutional* law of Massachusetts" and averring, "it is no triumph of faction, but of the people. The result of no momentary impulse but of the fixed and determined principle of the people to defend their rights and honor."

Local commentary on the decision to remove Loring was similarly divided. The *Liberator* proclaimed that removal "elicits the warmest congratulations from the friends of freedom universally." Similarly, dismissing concerns about judicial independence as "the merest twaddle and moonshine," the *Boston Bee* declared that Banks's actions "vindicated [the dignity of Massachusetts,] proved her power, and placed her where she has always proudly and firmly stood, on the side of law, justice, and humanity."

However, by its own account, the *Bee* stood almost alone among local commentators in endorsing Banks's decision. Loring himself provided one of the most detailed critiques of the decision to remove him from office. In addition to reiterating his view that section 14 of the personal liberty law unconstitutionally threatened judicial independence, Loring excoriated Banks for not exercising his right to consult the Supreme Judicial Court on the issue before making his decision.

Loring also defended his decision to rely on his personal judgment that the statute was unconstitutional, observing, "the refusal to obey an unconstitutional statute is the only lawful means by which its constitutionality can be determined and exposed." If the legislature disagreed, he contended, then he should have been impeached and tried for malfeasance rather than being removed under the petition and address provision.

A number of Boston newspapers also criticized the decision to remove Loring. For example, although the *Daily Advertiser* praised the "calm and statesmanlike view of the case taken [by Governor Banks]," it characterized the removal as "the result of a *prejudice* unfounded in any basis of sound policy, and unjust to the individual against whom it has been directed." More hyperbolically, the *Boston Post* condemned the removal as "the worst political deed that Massachusetts has seen since her ratification of the Federal Constitution" and complained that Banks had acted at the behest of "a radical and fanatical herd of abolitionists," and the *Boston Courier* asserted that "all men who are not blinded by a mistaken fanaticism, express themselves in fitting terms respecting the outrage which has been committed upon the independence of the judiciary and the wound that has been inflicted upon the body of the Constitution."

Sentiment against removal was even more one-sided outside Massachusetts. To be sure, abolitionist newspapers hailed the decision. For example, the *National Anti-Slavery Standard* declared that the state of Massachusetts "has secured its rights, and prevented the curses of posterity from being heaped upon its memory," while the *National Era* described the complaints about removal as "ridiculous." But such views were in the distinct minority. Not surprisingly, much of the harshest criticism came from the slave states. Thus, on the floor of the House of Representatives, Hugh Maynard of Tennessee characterized Loring's removal as "the latest act in the drama of fanaticism" from Boston, and a committee formed to set the agenda for a Southern convention to meet in Montgomery proclaimed, "the State of Massachusetts has perpetrated an act such as was never committed before by any Constitutional government." Southern newspaper commentary was equally emphatic. The *Baltimore American* asserted that removal had dealt "a radical and fatal blow aimed at the independence of the judiciary," while the *Fayetteville Observer* of North Carolina labeled

Banks's decision "an outrage" and the *Virginia Free Press* declared that removal "was an act of fanaticism, which would nullify the laws of the land." Similarly, a correspondent in the *Richmond South* sneered that, "to her eternal disgrace, Massachusetts is the first State in the Confederacy whose Legislature, too cowardly to assert its fancied rights against the national government by secession or otherwise, wreaks its vengeance against the individual sworn to execute the law, and endeavors to set the interests of the man in opposition to his official duty." Northern Democratic organs were equally unsparing in their criticism. The *National Intelligencer* characterized the removal decision as "an act of political intolerance and injustice which inflicts deep reproach on the elevated character of Massachusetts," and the *New York Courier* asserted that the decision was "animated by a vindictive, venomous spirit."

But perhaps most striking was the criticism from Republican journals. Although the Boston correspondent of the *New York Times* described Banks's message as "a capital state paper" demonstrating that Banks "is well up to his work," the *Times* itself declared that "a principle has been violated in [Loring's] vindictive removal that good citizens are wont to regard as sacred," and it predicted that "[Banks] will regret the step [he has] taken." The *Providence Journal* expressed similar sentiments, and the *Newark Daily Advertiser* characterized removal as "an unjust act of party malevolence."

In any event, the loss of his probate judgeship ultimately did not prove to be a major professional setback for Loring himself. On April 29, 1858, the death of John J. Gilchrist created a vacancy on the federal Court of Claims, and a number of Democratic representatives and senators, seeking to rebuke "the fanaticism of Massachusetts," urged President James Buchanan to appoint Loring to fill the vacancy. Buchanan quickly acceded to this request, and on May 6 Loring was confirmed by the Senate on a vote of 27–13. Loring served without controversy on the Court of Claims until his retirement on December 14, 1877.

Loring died in 1890. He was remembered as "a man of charming personality, a raconteur of the very highest order. He, with his wife and daughters, each brilliant and witty, rendered the Loring home (in Washington) a centre of social delight, unsurpassed elsewhere in Washington."

Conclusion

The difficulties faced by Edward Loring in 1854 can be traced to a variety of forces. On a macro political level, these difficulties were a by-product of the ongoing deterioration in sectional relations that marked the political climate of the 1850s. The conflict between the radical antislavery forces and the conservatives who favored sectional accommodation for the sake of maintaining the Union had long been a significant force in Massachusetts politics, particularly within the Whig Party. However, the struggle over the Compromise of 1850 and the resentment over the Kansas-Nebraska Act provided impetus to the antislavery forces, and accommodationists such as Loring were increasingly isolated.

Against this background, the Anthony Burns case presented Loring with one of the most basic dilemmas encountered by any jurist. He was forced to decide how a judge should proceed when confronted with a fundamentally unjust law. Loring's critics suggested a number of courses of action. For example, he might have resigned rather than participate in the enforcement of such a law, or he might have committed himself from the outset to adopt any plausible theory that would have prevented Burns's rendition. But Loring's conception of the role of a jurist was quite different. He believed that it was his duty to evaluate the law and the facts objectively and to implement that evaluation, even if the result might seem unjust in the abstract.

Subsequently, during the removal hearings, Richard Henry Dana would implicitly characterize this approach as evidence of a basic character flaw. Dana argued that Loring had ordered the rendition of Anthony Burns because "Judge Loring has none of those strong instincts in favor of justice and humanity, which . . . have gradually changed the jurisprudence of England from a system of tyranny to a system of liberty." But Loring, no doubt, would have argued that he was demonstrating a different kind of moral courage by dispassionately analyzing the demands of the Fugitive Slave Act in the face of strong public pressure to discharge Burns rather than return him to the custody of his erstwhile master. By doing so, Loring would have argued, he was vindicating the concept of the rule of law that undergirds the proper functioning of the legal system.

In short, the choices Edward Loring faced were a microcosm of those that confronted Northerners generally in the mid- and late 1850s. For many, the question was whether the integrity of their governing institutions should be maintained even at the expense of providing aid and comfort to the institution of slavery. Ultimately, only the Civil War would answer the question definitively.

CHRONOLOGY

1787   Adoption of the Fugitive Slave Clause by the Constitutional Convention.

1789   Ratification of the Constitution.

1793   Passage of first federal Fugitive Slave Act.

1802   Birth of Edward Greely Loring.

1823   Supreme Judicial Court of Massachusetts rejects constitutional challenge to Fugitive Slave Act in *Commonwealth v. Griffith*.

1833   Birth of Anthony Burns.

1836   *Chickasaw* affair.

1837   Massachusetts legislature reinstates writ of personal replevin.

1842   U.S. Supreme Court rejects constitutional challenge to Fugitive Slave Act in *Prigg v. Pennsylvania*; effort to reclaim George Latimer ends with Bostonians purchasing his freedom.

1843   Massachusetts passes personal liberty law.

1847   Edward Loring named probate judge for Suffolk County, Massachusetts.

1850   Adoption of Fugitive Slave Act of 1850; formation of Vigilance Committee in Boston; William and Ellen Craft escape effort to reclaim them.

1851   Rescue of Shadrach Minkins; unsuccessful effort to strengthen Massachusetts personal liberty law; rendition of Thomas Sims; Supreme Judicial Court of Massachusetts rejects constitutional challenge to Fugitive Slave Act in *Sims* case.

1851–1852   Unsuccessful prosecution of participants in the rescue of Shadrach Minkins.

1852   Edward Loring joins Harvard faculty.

1854   Introduction and passage of Kansas-Nebraska Act; escape, attempted rescue, and rendition of Anthony Burns; killing of James Batchelder; sale of Burns by Charles Suttle to David McDaniel; Henry Gardner elected governor of Massachusetts; Know-Nothings take control of state legislature.

1854–1855   Unsuccessful prosecution of participants in the effort to rescue Burns.

1855   Purchase of Burns's freedom; Loring loses position at Harvard; legislature votes to remove Loring from his position as probate judge, but Gardner refuses to acquiesce; passage of Personal Liberty Law of 1855; Gardner reelected governor.

1856   Gardner reelected governor; Republicans take control of state legislature.

1857   Legislature votes again to remove Loring, but Gardner again refuses to acquiesce; Nathaniel Banks elected governor.

1858   Loring removed from probate judgeship and appointed judge of the federal Court of Claims.

1862   Death of Anthony Burns.

1877   Loring retires from Court of Claims.

1890   Death of Edward Loring.

BIBLIOGRAPHICAL ESSAY

Note from the Series Editors: The following bibliographic essay contains the major primary and secondary sources the author consulted for this volume. We have asked all authors in the series to omit formal citations in order to make our volumes more readable, inexpensive, and appealing for students and general readers. In adopting this format, Landmark Law Cases and American Society follows the precedent of a number of highly regarded and widely consulted series.

This treatment of the Anthony Burns affair and the subsequent removal of Edward Loring is based on both primary and secondary sources. Contemporary newspaper accounts were invaluable. Many of these accounts can be found in two important databases: the *American Periodical Series Online, 1740–1900*, and *Nineteenth Century American Newspapers*. The *Liberator* and the *Boston Daily Advertiser* were among the most consistently useful sources. These newspapers not only were exemplars of the abolitionist and conservative Whig perspectives, respectively, but also provided detailed accounts of the actions of the Massachusetts legislature, including committee hearings and reports. As the text indicates, other newspapers presented different political viewpoints. For example, the *Springfield Republican* reflected the thoughts of moderate antislavery forces, while the *Boston Post* and *Boston Journal* were organs of the Democratic Party.

Periodicals based outside of Massachusetts demonstrated the impact of developments there on the political culture of the nation more generally. Publications such as the *National Anti-Slavery Standard*, *National Era*, and *New York Tribune* chronicled the reactions of radical opponents of slavery to events in Massachusetts; the *New York Times* hewed to the position of moderate antislavery Whigs and Republicans; and the *New York Journal of Commerce* and *National Intelligencer* embodied the views of Northerners who were more sympathetic to Southern concerns. Not surprisingly, mainstream Southern newspapers such as the *Richmond Examiner*, *Fayetteville (NC) Observer*, and *Daily South Carolinian* were more united in their approach to issues related to fugitive slaves.

Among secondary sources, Charles Emery Stevens, *Anthony Burns: A History* (Boston: John P. Jewett, 1856), gives a detailed account of the Burns affair, related largely by Burns himself. "The Boston Slave Riot, and Trial of Anthony Burns," in *Fugitive Slaves and American Courts: The Pamphlet Literature*, ed. Paul Finkelman (New York: Garland Publishing, 1988), vol. 2, 343–428, also describes many of the critical events that culminated in Burns's rendition. The best-known modern treatment of the affair is Albert J. Von Franck, *The Trials of Anthony Burns: Freedom and Slavery in Emerson's Boston*

(Boston: Harvard University Press, 1997). David Russell Maginnes, "The Point of Honor: The Rendition of the Fugitive Slave Anthony Burns, Boston, 1854" (doctoral dissertation, Columbia University, 1973), is richly detailed and more straightforward than Von Franck's work. Jane H. Pease and William H. Pease, *The Fugitive Slave Law and Anthony Burns: A Problem in Law Enforcement* (Boston: Lippincott, 1975), is also useful, as is Paul Finkelman, "Legal Ethics and Fugitive Slaves: The Anthony Burns Case, Judge Loring, and Abolitionist Attorneys," *Cardozo Law Review* 17 (1996): 1793–1858. Although all these works pay some attention to the removal of Edward Loring, the most complete treatment is Kevin L. Gilbert, "The Ordeal of Edward Greely Loring: Fugitive Slavery, Judicial Reform, and the Politics of Law in 1850s Massachusetts" (doctoral dissertation, State University of New York–Albany, 1997).

The account of passage of the Fugitive Slave Act of 1793 is taken from Earl M. Maltz, *The Supreme Court and Slavery: 1825–1861* (Lawrence: University Press of Kansas, 2009), which in turn relied on Paul Finkelman, "The Kidnapping of John Davis and the Adoption of the Fugitive Slave Law of 1793," *Journal of Southern History* 56 (1990): 397–422, and William R. Leslie, "A Study in the Origins of Interstate Rendition: The Big Beaver Creek Murders," *American Historical Review* 57 (1951): 63–76. The *Chickasaw* affair is chronicled in Leonard Levy, *The Law of the Commonwealth and Chief Justice Shaw* (Cambridge, MA: Harvard University Press, 1957), 73–77, and reinstatement of the writ of personal replevin in Massachusetts is described in Thomas D. Morris, *Free Men All: The Personal Liberty Laws of the North, 1780–1861* (Baltimore: Johns Hopkins University Press, 1974).

The discussion of *Prigg v. Pennsylvania* is also taken from Maltz, *The Supreme Court and Slavery*. The text of the decision itself can be found in the official reports at 41 U.S. (16 Pet.) 539 (1842). For other perspectives, see Joseph C. Burke, "What Did the Prigg Decision Really Decide," *Pennsylvania Magazine of History and Biography* 93 (1969): 80; Paul Finkelman, "Story Telling on the Supreme Court: *Prigg v. Pennsylvania* and Justice Joseph Story's Judicial Nationalism," *Supreme Court Review* (1994): 247–294; Morris, *Free Men All*, 94–107; R. Kent Newmyer, *Supreme Court Justice Joseph Story: Statesman of the Old Republic* (Chapel Hill: University of North Carolina Press, 1985), 370–375; Barbara Holden Smith, "Lords of Lash, Loom, and Law: Justice Story, Slavery, and *Prigg v. Pennsylvania*," *Cornell Law Review* 78 (1993): 1086–1151; and Carl B. Swisher, *History of the Supreme Court*, vol. 5, *The Taney Period* (New York: Macmillan, 1974), 535–547.

Latimer and passage of the Personal Liberty Law of 1843 are discussed in Levy, *The Law of the Commonwealth and Chief Justice Shaw*, 78–85, and Morris, *Free Men All*, 109–112. Shaw's decision is described in the *Liberator*, November 4, 1842. Contemporary reactions to resolution of the rendition effort can be found in "House No. 41, February, 1843, Joint Special Committee of the Senate and House of Representatives of the State of Massachusetts, to Whom Was Referred the Petition of George Latimer," in Finkelman, *Fugitive Slaves and American Courts*, vol. 1, 177–210, and "Proceedings of the Borough of Norfolk, on the Boston Outrage, in the Case of the Runaway Slave George Latimer," ibid., 211–230.

Discussion of the evolution of the Fugitive Slave Act of 1850 is taken from Maltz, *The Supreme Court and Slavery*, which relied heavily on the accounts in Stanley W. Campbell, *The Slave Catchers: Enforcement of the Fugitive Slave Law, 1850–1860* (Chapel Hill: University of North Carolina Press, 1968), 15–25; William W. Freehling, *The Road to Disunion*, vol. 1, *Secessionists at Bay* (New York: Oxford University Press, 1990), 501–505; and Morris, *Free Men All*, 132–145.

A number of the major players in the radical antislavery movement in Massachusetts have been the subjects of informative biographies. For information on the life and views of Wendell Phillips, see James Brewer Stewart, *Wendell Phillips, Liberty's Hero* (Baton Rouge: Louisiana State University Press, 1986), and Irving H. Bartlett, *Wendell Phillips, Brahmin Radical* (Boston: Beacon Press, 1961). Important studies of Theodore Parker include Dean Grodzins, *American Heretic: Theodore Parker and Transcendentalism* (Chapel Hill: University of North Carolina Press, 2002), and John Edward Dirks, *The Critical Theology of Theodore Parker* (Westport, CT: Greenwood Press, 1970). Richard Henry Dana is the subject of Samuel Shapiro, *Richard Henry Dana, Jr., 1815–1882* (East Lansing: Michigan State University Press, 1961). In addition, Robert R. Lucid, ed., *The Journal of Richard Henry Dana, Jr.*, 3 vols. (Cambridge, MA: Harvard University Press, 1968), provides an indispensable contemporaneous account of many of the relevant events.

Among conservatives, Daniel Webster is the subject of a massive literature. For purposes of this book, I found Maurice G. Baxter, *One and Inseparable: Daniel Webster and the Union* (Cambridge, MA: Harvard University Press, 1984), and Robert Dalzell, *Daniel Webster and the Trial of American Nationalism* (Boston: Houghton Mifflin, 1973), particularly useful. The approach of Justice Benjamin Robbins Curtis is examined in Stuart Streichler, *Justice Curtis in the Civil War Era: At the Crossroads of American Constitutionalism* (Charlottesville: University of Virginia Press, 2005). In addition, see Earl M. Maltz, "The Unlikely Hero of Dred Scott: Benjamin R. Curtis and the Constitutional Law of Slavery," *Cardozo Law Review* 17 (1996): 1995–2016.

The attempt to recapture the Crafts is chronicled in R. J. M. Blackett, "The Odyssey of William and Ellen Craft," in *Beating against the Barriers: Biographical Essays in Nineteenth Century African-American History* (Ithaca, NY: Cornell University Press, 1986), 87–137, and Gary Collison, *Shadrach Minkins: From Fugitive Slave to Citizen* (Cambridge, MA: Harvard University Press, 1997), 91–101. As one might expect, the latter also discusses the Shadrach

Minkins rescue in detail. A transcript of the proceedings against one of those charged with participating in the rescue effort can be found at "*United States v. Charles G. Davis*. Report of the Proceedings at the Examination of Charles G. Davis, Esq., on a Charge of Aiding and Abetting in the Rescue of a Fugitive Slave, Held in Boston, in February, 1851," in Finkelman, *Fugitive Slaves and American Courts*, vol. 1, 573–616.

The rendition of Thomas Sims is discussed in detail in Leonard Levy, "Sims' Case: The Fugitive Slave Law in Boston in 1851," *Journal of Negro History* 35 (1950): 39–74. Briefer accounts can be found in Campbell, *The Slave Catchers*, 99–100, 118–120, and Morris, *Free Men All*, 151–153. The arguments of Sims's counsel, together with the decision of George Ticknor Curtis, are reproduced in "The Trial of Thomas Sims, on an Issue of Personal Liberty, on the Claim of James Potter, of Georgia, against Him, as an Alleged Fugitive from Service," in Finkelman, *Fugitive Slaves and American Courts*, vol. 1, 617–664. Shaw's decision on the petition for the writ of habeas corpus can be found in the official Massachusetts reports at 7 Cushing 285 (1851).

In addition to the monographs that focus on the rendition of Anthony Burns, the case is considered at some length in Campbell, *The Slave Catchers*, 124–131, and Morris, *Free Men All*, 166–168, which emphasizes the impact of the Kansas-Nebraska Act on public opinion in Boston. For a detailed discussion of the adoption of the Personal Liberty Law of 1855, see ibid., 168–173.

Benjamin Robbins Curtis's charge to the grand jury considering indictments against those who participated in the abortive rescue effort can be found in Benjamin R. Curtis Jr., ed., *A Memoir of Benjamin Robbins Curtis, L.L.D., with Some of His Professional and Miscellaneous Writings*, 2 vols. (New York: Da Capo Press, 1970), 2:205–212. Edward R. Hoar's charge to the grand jury in the Boston municipal court is reproduced in "Charge to the Grand Jury at the July Term of the Municipal Court in Boston, 1854," in Finkelman, *Fugitive Slaves and American Courts*, vol. 2, 469–490. Theodore Parker, *The Trial of Theodore Parker: For the Misdemeanor of a Speech in Faneuil Hall against Kidnapping, before the Circuit Court of the United States at Boston, April 3, 1855*, can be found online at http://www.ebooksread.com/authors-eng/theodore-parker/the-trial-of-theodore-parker-for-the-misdemeanor-of-a-speech-in-faneuil-hall-hci.shtml. The proceedings in an unsuccessful tort action against those who were charged with keeping order during Burns's transfer from the courthouse to the ship are reproduced in Finkelman, *Fugitive Slaves and American Courts*, vol. 3, 313–330.

The official documents and main arguments generated in the struggle to remove Edward Loring are compiled in Finkelman, *Fugitive Slaves and American Courts*, vol. 3. Carla Bosca, "Harvard and the Fugitive Slave Act," *New England Quarterly* 79 (2006): 227–247; Finkelman, "Legal Ethics and Fugitive Slaves," chronicles the university's refusal to reappoint Loring; and Louis A.

Frothingham, "The Removal of Judges by Judicial Address in Massachusetts," *American Political Science Review* 8 (1914): 216–221, discusses the history of the state constitutional provision invoked against Loring.

Tyler Anbinder, *Nativism and Slavery: The Northern Know Nothings and the Politics of the 1850s* (New York: Oxford University Press, 1992), and William Gienapp, *Origins of the Republican Party, 1852–1857* (New York: Oxford University Press, 1987), analyze the relationship among the Know-Nothing movement, the campaign against slavery, and the rise of the Republican Party. Dale Baum, *The Civil War Party System: The Case of Massachusetts, 1848–1876* (Chapel Hill: University of North Carolina Press, 1984), and John R. Mulkern, *The Know Nothing Party of Massachusetts: The Rise and Fall of a People's Movement* (Boston: Northeastern University Press, 1990), focus on the complex political situation in Massachusetts in the mid-1850s. Useful biographies of central figures in the Massachusetts conflict include Richard H. Abbott, *Cobbler in Congress: The Life of Henry Wilson, 1812–1875* (Lexington: University Press of Kentucky, 1975); John M. Belohlavek, *Broken Glass: Caleb Cushing and the Shattering of the Union* (Kent, OH: Kent State University Press, 2005); and James G. Hollandsworth Jr., *Pretense of Glory: The Life of General Nathaniel G. Banks* (Baton Rouge: Louisiana State University Press, 1998).

INDEX

Fugitive slaves, 1, 4, 24, 31, 40, 101, 137
  controversy over, 10, 16, 19, 26, 53,
    54
  harboring/concealing, 9, 10, 87
  recovery of, 6, 7, 8–9, 10, 19, 21–22,
    25, 27, 130
  rendition of, 8, 9, 11, 13, 29
  rights of, 14, 35
Full Faith and Credit Clause, 74, 82,
  86

Gardner, Henry J., 113
  antislavery cause and, 112, 137, 138
  fusion movement and, 137, 138
  Know-Nothing Party and, 112, 138,
    144–145
  Loring removal and, 131, 132–133,
    134, 138, 139–140, 143–144, 145,
    153
  personal liberty law and, 134, 138
Gardnerites, 145, 148
Garrison, William Lloyd, 67, 130, 149,
    151
Gilchrist, John J., 156
Gitchell, John W., 120
Gould, Cyrus, 77
Gould, Erasmus, 126
Gould, Erastus B., 77
Gradual Emancipation Act (1780), 7
Gray, James B., 22–23, 24
Greenough, William, 105
Griffin, J. Q. A., 138
Griffith, Camillus, 11
Grimes, Leonard A., 58, 118
  purchasing Burns freedom and, 2, 9,
    66, 67, 68, 70, 71, 90, 95, 96, 98,
    119, 123, 127

Habeas corpus, 11–12, 13, 22, 26, 36, 40,
    42, 43, 44, 46, 51, 54
Hale, Charles, 142, 151–152
Hale, John P., 27, 38, 52, 53, 104, 136
Hale, Sir Matthew, 78
Hallett, Benjamin, 32, 45, 49, 50, 67,
    76, 78, 84, 101
  Butman and, 103
  Davis charges and, 39
  Ellis exchange with, 72
  fugitive slave cases and, 54
  indictments and, 105, 106
  Loring decision and, 90

militia and, 85
purchasing Burns freedom and, 68,
    71, 74–75, 91, 96
trial and, 104
Ham, Luther A., 66
Harvard Corporation, 109, 110
Harvard Law School, 1, 57, 70, 109
Hayden, Lewis, 39, 52, 61, 62, 63, 64,
    100
Hayes, Joseph K., 91, 92
Henderson, Thomas, 17
Higginson, Thomas Whitworth, 61,
    62, 63, 64, 101, 103
Hildreth, Richard, 44, 120
Hilliard, George F., 145
Hoar, Ebenezer R., 101–102, 103
Hoar, George, 103
Hoar, Samuel, 103
Howe, Samuel Gridley, 61, 62, 109
Hughes, Willis H., 31, 32, 33

Impeachment, 113, 114, 117, 125, 131,
    135, 140, 143, 155
Innes, James, 7–8
Irish Catholics, 112
Izard, Ralph, 9

Jamestown (steamer), 95
Johnston, Samuel, 9
Joint Special Committee, 39
Joint Standing Committee on Federal
    Relations, 134, 140
Jones, William, 76, 77, 82, 92–93
Judicial independence, 116, 121, 126,
    140, 143, 151, 155
Judiciary Committee, 14, 26, 148

Kansas-Nebraska Act (1854), 54, 65,
    68, 111, 136
  condemnation of, 2, 112, 157
Kemp, Henry, 61, 62, 63
Kennedy, James, 25
Kimball, Eben, 129
Knowles, Elijah E., 125
Know-Nothing Party, 119, 131, 137, 139,
    144–145
  antislavery movement and, 113, 138
  fusion movement and, 138
  nativism and, 111, 112
  Republican Party and, 136, 144, 145
  slavery and, 111, 136

170